WHEATON PUBLIC LIBRARY

3 5143 00495472 0

P9-BYE-021

PLANTING THE COUNTRY WAY

A Hands-on Approach

PLANTING THE COUNTRY WAY

A Hands-on Approach

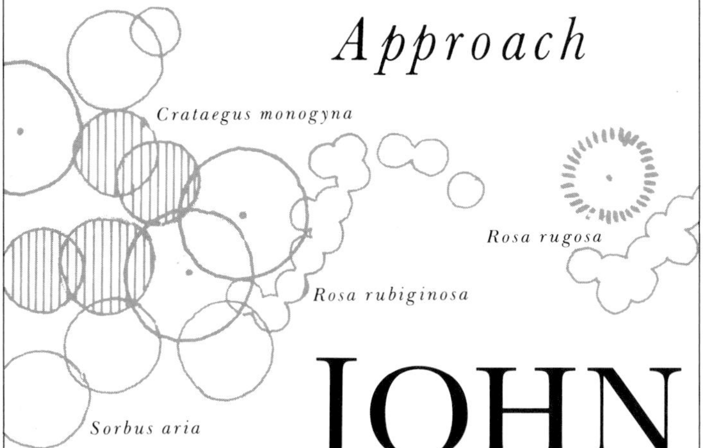

Crataegus monogyna

Rosa rugosa

Rosa rubiginosa

Sorbus aria

JOHN BROOKES

BBC BOOKS

Photographs of the following gardens are featured in this book.

Page 13: Denmans, Sussex. Designer: John Brookes.

Pages 44–5: Cottage garden at Steeple Aston, Oxford.

Page 57: Hestercombe, Somerset, by kind permission of the Somerset Fire Brigade.

Pages 58–63: Cottage at Dolton, Devon.
Designer: Cathy Taylor.

Pages 94–5: Waterperry Gardens, Wheatley, Oxford.

Pages 96–7: Ashton, Northampton, by kind permission of the Hon. Mrs M. L. Lane.

Pages 100–1: Old Rectory, Tidmarsh, Berkshire, by kind permission of Bill and Joan Baker.

Pages 102–3: Vann, Surrey, by kind permission of Mr & Mrs Martin Caroe.

Pages 112–15: Private cottage, Devon.

Pages 116–21: Wilderness Farm, Kent.
Designer: Ryl Nowell.

Pages 124–8: Eastgrove Cottage, Sankyns Green, Worcestershire. Designers: Malcolm and Carol Skinner.

Pages 130–3: Private garden, Northamptonshire.
Designer: Dan Pearson.

Pages 134–5: Private garden, Sussex.
Designer: John Brookes.

Pages 142–9: Denmans, Sussex.
Designer: John Brookes.

Pages 152–7: Stone Farm, Chagford, Devon.
Designers: Kenneth and June Ashburner.

Pages 158–61: Private garden, Sussex.
Designer: Mrs Louise Trépanier.

Pages 164–9: Private garden, Oxfordshire.
Designers: Michael and Denny Wickham.

Previous spread: Green-flowering *Euphorbia amygdaloides* 'Rubra' with *Verbascum olympicum* – only one remove from our native wood spurge and great mullein.

Published by BBC Books,
a division of BBC Enterprises Limited,
Woodlands, 80 Wood Lane, London W12 0TT

First published 1994
© John Brookes 1994

ISBN 0 563 36799 7

Designed by Harry Green

Set in Baskerville by Selwood Systems,
Midsomer Norton
Printed and bound in Great Britain
by Butler & Tanner Ltd, Frome and London
Colour separations by Radstock Reproductions,
Midsomer Norton
Jacket printed by Lawrence Allen Ltd,
Weston Super Mare

BBC Books would like to thank the following for providing photographs, and for permission to reproduce copyright material. While every effort has been made to trace and acknowledge all copyright holders, we would like to apologize should there have been any errors or omissions

KEY T = TOP B = BELOW L = LEFT R = RIGHT

JOHN BROOKES pages 1, 16–17 (Weald & Downland Museum), 26, 46–47, 49, 51T,B, 61, 66–67, 69, 70–71T, 76L, 80–81, 82, 85, 88, 89, 104–105, 115, 117, 124, 127, 139T,BL,BR, 148L, 172, 173;
LIZ EDDISON pages 11, 106–107 (Chelsea 94), 174–175 (Chelsea 90);
EDIFICE/DARLEY page 64–65;
FLPA/J. HUTCHINGS page 32–33;
THE GARDEN PICTURE LIBRARY/STEVEN WOOSTER page 72–73;
JOHN GLOVER pages 34–35, 74–75;
NADA JENNET pages 54, 55;
ANDREW LAWSON pages 3, 9, 10, 13, 14–15, 18, 20, 22, 24–25, 31, 36L, 36R–37, 38–39, 40, 41T,B, 42L, 43T,B, 44–45, 48, 57, 58–59, 62–63, 70–71B, 76R–77, 78–79, 92, 93, 94–95, 96–97, 98–99, 100–101, 102–103, 108–109, 110–111, 112, 114–115L, 118–119, 120–121, 122L,R, 125, 126, 130, 131, 132–133, 134, 135, 142L, 142R–143, 144L, 144R–145, 148R–149, 151T,B, 152R–153, 154–155, 156, 157T, 158L, 158R–159, 161T,B, 164L, 164R–165, 167, 168L, 168R–169;
THE MUSEUM OF MODERN ART, NEW YORK/GIFT OF MRS & MRS BURTON TREMAINE page 68–69;
NATIONAL TRUST PHOTOGRAPHIC LIBRARY/JOE CORNISH page 28–29;
NKPA/E. A. JANES page 32–33.

ACKNOWLEDGEMENTS

I have been probably been boring my gardening friends – not to mention my students – for some time now with my theories and I would like to thank them all for their forbearance.

I would also thank my assistant Michael Zinn, and Caroline Egremont with whom he works; both have helped in providing drawings and doing valuable research. Also my secretary Jill Robertson-Macdonald for interpreting and putting on screen my handwritten scrawl.

I have been conscious of the work and writings of The Hon. Miriam Rothschild for a number of years, for she was working early in the field of an interest in wild flowers. I am grateful for her gracious preface to the book.

Garden-owners and designers have been unfailingly helpful. I would like to thank them in alphabetical order.

Mr and Mrs K. Ashburner
Mr and Mrs I. Cahn
Miss Kay Fairfax
Mr and Mrs G. Ferguson
Mr and Mrs F. Joyce
Mr and Mrs N. Lutte
Mrs Ryl Nowell
Mr Daniel Pearson
Mr and Mrs J. W. Robertson
Mr Trevor Scott
Mr and Mrs M. Skinner
Mr and Mrs Ray Taylor
Mr W. J. Tooby
Mrs Louise Trèpanier
Mr and Mrs Michael Wickham

Lastly, Tessa Clark, who has edited down my script, and Harry Green who has laid out the book – both have been hugely supportive. Andrew Lawson not only provided his own garden but sumptuous photographs of many more. I thank them most warmly.

PREFACE

Opposite page:
The Hon. Miriam
Rothschild, naturalist
and gardener, in her
Northamptonshire
garden.

Although many of our garden flowers and vegetables have been improved and altered by selection, crossing, grafting and skilled environmental changes, they still are, in some parts of the world, wild flowers. This was brought home to me forcibly when I first saw clumps of snow-white arum lilies growing alongside roads in New Zealand and black-eye Susans adorning the verges in Texas.

I decided to try and mix both the local flora and the more gaudy foreign flowers in my garden. The uncut lawns surrounding my house were first selected for this experiment. This is not a challenge to the traditional flowering hayfield with its sheets of yellow buttercups and twinkling ox-eye daisies – it is a completely different concept showing – I hoped – how naturally exotic flowers and cultivated flowers can mix with each other and our own native plants in perfect harmony in the garden.

I am, at heart, a dedicated grass gardener. Plants have evolved flowers to attract insect and bird pollinators, but the grasses are wind pollenated and have conquered the world. Can anything be more beautiful than quaking grass or wild oats or wall barley or Yorkshire fog? I only have to cut the grass once a year, in late September and October. In the spring before it begins to grow vigorously, snowdrops are unrivalled, but later, when 'the lawn' is about eighteen inches high, patches of snowflakes take their place; simultaneously I grow several white tulips which look wonderful in long grass and the lavender and yellow *Bakerei* (lilac wonder) catch the spring sunshine, as they spread their petals along the edges of the one strip of lawn which is mown in a conventional manner.

There is really no end to the species you can try, from anemones to globe flowers and gladioli. I am very keen on the numerous species of *Allium*, which can hold their own in long grass, and I plant them together with Dutch iris (yellow, white and mauve), which are followed by the English iris and finally, towards the end of July, various lilies (pink, yellow and white), which shine just above the late beige grasses.

When visitors turn up at my house, they look around at the tangle of creepers which completely hide the stonework from view and pause, puzzled – surely, no one can live here !?

I unhesitatingly grow wild and garden flowers together, all over the house – wild roses are planted alongside Kiftsgate and the climbing Étoile. Montana clematis competes with our native species, old man's beard. Buddleia reaches the rooftops. In the middle of the courtyard I have planted pear and plum trees, bullace, wild and Japanese cherries and various continental *Prunus*. To me, at least, this confusion of the wild and the tame seems completely natural. It isn't really a muddle, for like Alfred Tennyson, I favour a 'careless ordered garden'. The greatest triumph was the evening when a nightingale visited the courtyard.

My outlook is really that of a naturalist. If you want to learn how to combine local wild flowers with exotic plants and at the same time take advantage of the local scenery – be it trees, water, hills or clouds – you must consult John Brookes' book. You will find it all there within the framework of a gardener's perceptive and intuitive design.

MIRIAM ROTHSCHILD

CONTENTS

INTRODUCTION

I have become increasingly more uncomfortable with what might be called 'the manicured garden'. In my mind I see a neat, suburban home – it could be anywhere in the country – surrounded by an overly striped lawn which is, of course, completely free of daisies. This green carpet has a knife edge – a sort of mini-cliff – with an earthy gap at the base before some planting. Roses possibly, or, as the dream turns to nightmare, neat little clumps of glaucous or gold conifer edged with heather. As it is April, unseasonal flowering heathers are backed by yolk-bright forsythia with, in the distance, the solitary form of a Japanese cherry. The poor lone thing is still flowering its sickly pink.

Familiar? Yes, very. And why am I so scathing when every year we welcome spring's return with just such plantings? The answer is that the conservationist's concern for the wild has got to me; I want to see the advent of spring through nature's eyes – the country way. I feel there has to be a coming together of tamed with wild. The latter, as it happens, is a misnomer both in terms of garden and country; plants are never tamed and what seems wild in Britain is far from that.

So what went wrong? When *did* gardeners retreat into their plots of hybrid-hued mini-plants and why have they rejected the gentler, natural approach?

Much is to do, I believe, with the given criteria. We have been fed a glossy diet of gardening techniques for large country houses on the one hand – and maintenance for vegetable plots on the other. The need to control plants by tool or spray is fed by horticultural advertising and has alienated many from nature. Plants must always be restricted, pruned and disciplined and grown in artificial clumps of three, five or seven.

Early man saw his garden as a retreat from the wild. Later, those who could afford decorative gardens had to establish their supremacy over untamed nature and gardens were controlled and formal, plants were clipped. Today, however, when the total area of private gardens is more than one million acres – not much less than that of all the special sites of scientific

Foxgloves are one of our most common biennials and are great self-seeders and wonderful plants for light shade. Here they are mixed with poppies and, beyond, yellow vetch – a flower of the cornfield.

interest – we should perhaps relax with our surroundings and even learn to work with them.

To do this we must select trees, shrubs and flowers from the abundance of garden plant material that is available, and try to use them in more natural surroundings.

My interest in a gentler design of garden planting started along these lines. Although I was brought up heir to the herbaceous border approach to using plants, this was far too artificial and too pat a solution to reconciling my material with

A garden which sits well within in its setting does not come to an abrupt halt at its boundary – there is a transition of the plantings of the layout outwards through looser, wilder groupings with longer grass, and any view that there is should be allowed to flow inwards.

the wild. I started to look at natural plant associations and, through them, at where they grew throughout the country. And this brought me to define the trees, shrubs and other vegetation that grows in a specific area.

I find that while most gardeners are very aware of their local climatic conditions and the acidity or alkalinity of their soil, their knowledge of their site stops there. I believe that with a growing preference for organic composts rather than chemical feeds and sprays, an increasing awareness of the wildlife that returns as a result of their use, and a general improvement in the quality of what grows, interest in the association between the topsoil, what is under it and the plants that originally grew on top of it (before exotics pushed them aside) will be strengthened and rekindled. We are learning to buck the international gardening scene and re-establish our regional roots through plantings that are more specific to their site.

We were, of course, always attached to the land; indeed, most of our ancestors made their livings from it. What I am interested in is whether this symbiosis can be re-created in our gardens. For an earthy concern for, and knowledge of, our surroundings is essential before we can start to furnish the gardens in their midst with plants whose selection and manner of planting is in keeping not only with nature's way, but with nature's way *in that particular spot.*

But progress is always made in the knowledge of the past; it is inevitably a reinterpretation of it – a 'natural' progression. Part of this progression is a new awareness of design in the garden. This is not at odds to my thesis – rather, it provides the setting to it. A designed garden is one that works for the family who uses it and the house it surrounds, whatever its scale or location. Its styling, in both construction and, more relatively, planting, is what links the layout to its site. For too long the merit of our gardens has been judged by the number of alien plants we

cram into them regardless of their surroundings. I believe that we can no longer afford this approach if we are to sustain our regional heritage.

This book seeks to amalgamate much current research and many facts from various disciplines such as geology, social history and ecology – all the elements of the patchwork of a landscape. In writing it I have shamelessly taken information from other authors, whom I would like to thank and whose authority I would like to acknowledge. I have therefore listed the books to which I referred in a bibliography at the end of the book. They make excellent further reading to what is, after all, a very complex subject.

LANDSCAPE AND PLANTING: A NATURAL HARMONY

Wherever you live in the country it is an area that originally had a particular type of vegetation that was specific to its altitude, weather, topography and soil – flowers, trees and shrubs that developed over the millennia as human beings adapted and refined the land and landscape to their pastoral lifestyle so that there was a harmony between man and nature.

A farmed landscape above Otmore in Oxfordshire would originally have been scrub and woodland of native trees.

OUR REGIONAL HERITAGE

Britain has a particular vernacular character, which changes every few miles – a result of the honing process whereby man worked the land and used its local resources of stone, clay or timber. The strong characteristics of each area are based upon its soil, from which grows a unique association of plant material. There is also a dependent range of animal, bird and insect life. Over the years man has introduced domestic breeds, adapted to the region and his requirements, within this rhythm or eco-system.

It is the sum total of all these aspects of a landscape that give it its regional identity – its look. And it is the strength of that heritage that it still survives despite our nineteenth- and twentieth-century incursions into it. But the look of a landscape is not a romantic association of the past; it lives and breathes right now and we are of it still. It only needs a thunderstorm, a snowfall or even a fine spring day to remind us that we are as subject to natural forces as are the flowers, trees and shrubs in our gardens.

Nevertheless, most of us have shed our close regional attachment to the land and many gardeners fill their plots with alien species. They will defy drought and winter chill to sustain their collections when surely it would be easier to cultivate the plants that grow nearer to home. For what grows locally does so with far less care and attention than more exotic plants and also helps to preserve the living cycle and regional identity that is our national heritage.

This is not a plea for growing only native material; rather it is one for taking a closer look at where we live and seeing how we can adapt our own piece of the wild.

A traditional cottage in West Sussex, with flintwork walling, is typical of its region.

TOPOGRAPHY AND TREES

Throughout the British Isles there are distinct geographical regions which are not defined by county – for these are man-made, determined by area rather than geography – and which are very different in character and mood. Much of this 'feel' is to do with topography, which defines whether land is flat and open like the fenlands of Lincolnshire, rolling wolds as in Leicestershire or fringe moorland as in Wales or on the slopes of the Pennines.

The regularity with which the landscape alters is due in great measure to the remarkable diversity of types and ages of rock which form the skeleton of the land. During the two million years

Wind and rain worked upon this landscape, which was probably quarried at one time for tin as well. Sheep then grazed over the remaining limestone and grit soil, its former shrub and tree cover long since depleted by numerous agencies.

Geology

The underlying rock formations of Britain and Ireland, shown in this map, have developed over many millenia. These formations, and the rivers and streams that run over and through them, broadly define our geographic regions and give a distinctive character to each one.

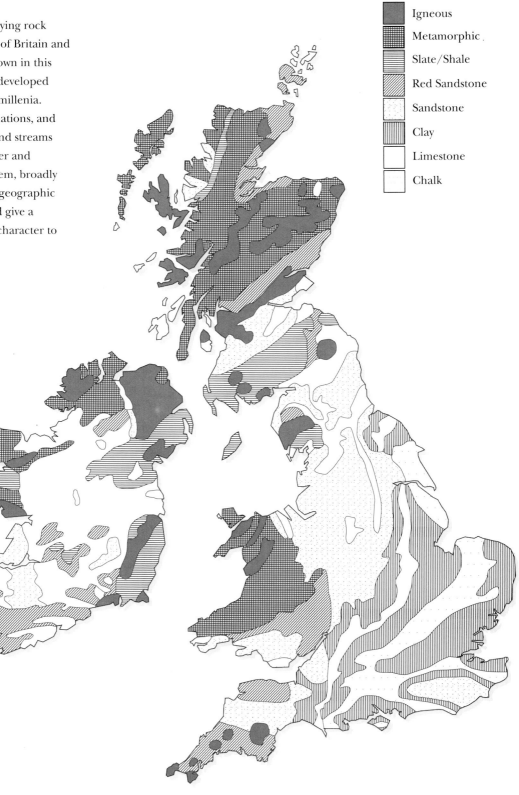

Igneous

Metamorphic

Slate/Shale

Red Sandstone

Sandstone

Clay

Limestone

Chalk

of the last ice age, this skeleton was further moulded by the ice sheets that covered northern Britain. The action of glaciers scoured the landscape and exaggerated the valley floors through which they passed. When the ice finally receded 10 000 years ago it left the deposits of boulder, clay and gravel that have dictated much of the shape of our landscape.

Over the millennia a combination of rain, wind, snow and sun broke down the surface of these original deposits into fine rock particles. These combined with water and organic matter to produce the different soils – and ultimately the different kinds of vegetation – that characterize the regions that can be broadly defined as heath-

land and moorland, open grasslands (including chalk downland), wetland, coastland and mountains. By far the greatest area, however, was native woodland.

As the chill of the ice receded, scrub and then trees started to grow from the rubble-strewn mosses and tundras and colonized the more hospitable of the developing regions. The first trees were small, cold-tolerant birches whose seed was spread by the wind, with dwarf willow and juniper. Then came larger birches and, in the south-east, pine woods. As the climate warmed, the pines and larger birches spread northwards with rowan and aspen, then hazel followed by alder and lime. Oak and wych elm colonized

Prevailing westerly winds create greater rainfall up the lefthand side of both the Irish land mass and that of West Country England, Wales, the Lake District and in Scotland. Agricultural areas tend to be in the east and south giving rise eventually to greater densities of population.

Rainfall

This map shows that there is a difference of as much as 2000 mm (78 in) between the driest and wettest regions in Britain and Ireland. These variations, and the effect of rain, sun and snow on differing geological formations has helped to define the different regions and hence their cultivation and agriculture.

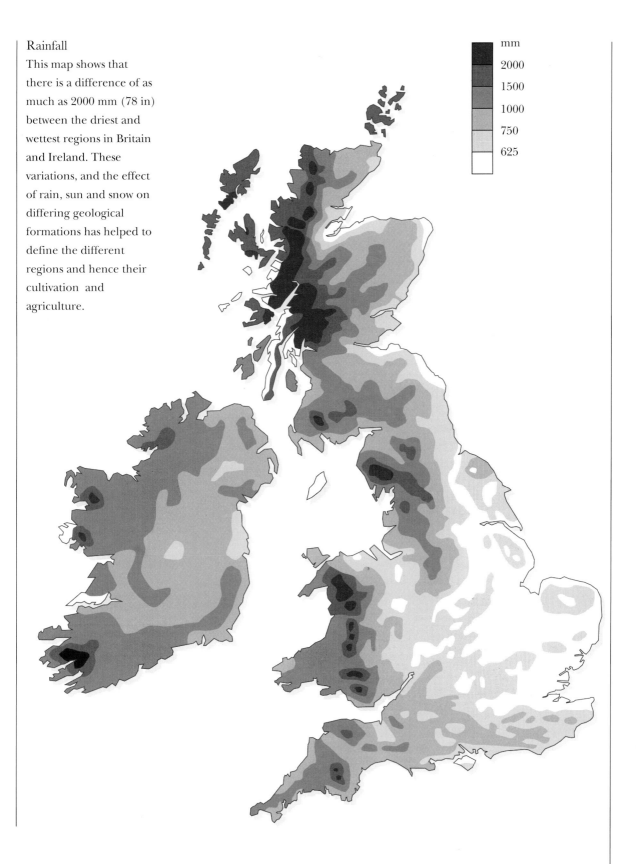

mm
2000
1500
1000
750
625

the south later and pine and oak reached Ireland. By the time England had split from France and then Holland great forests of lime, oak, elm, hazel and alder had been established, with later areas of beech, ash and maple. As Britain became moister its native wildwood expanded to cover at least two-thirds of the country. Local soils and climate determined the mix of plant material. The north and west of England and the Scottish lowlands were dominated by oak and hazel. Later plant arrivals expanded the growth. Beech grew on the freely drained chalk and gravel locations of well-drained downland and hornbeam displaced lime trees in the clay Thames basin.

The shape of a single gnarled hawthorn (*Crataegus monogyna*) follows the profile of the Cornish hillside beyond, both moulded by strong winds off the sea. The hawthorn sits in the West Country wall which was probably totally planted on top at one time to shelter stock.

Topography

The landscapes of Britain and Ireland were moulded primarily by the geology of the different regions, but also by the action of glaciers many thousands of years ago. This map shows how most of the areas of highest altitude are clustered towards the north where glaciers created deep valley floors as they carved their way through mountains.

heights in metres

1000
400
200
100
0

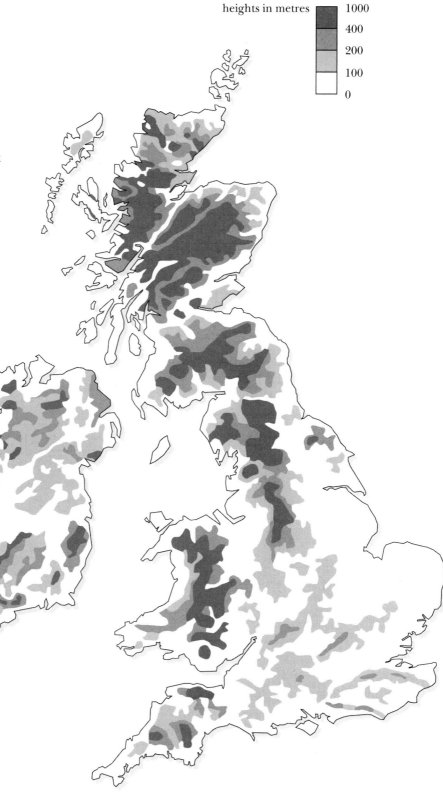

THE EVOLUTION OF OUR LANDSCAPE

As man and his agriculture developed he encroached into the ancient wildwoods. Between 1000 BC and 750 BC Britain's annual temperature dropped by about 2°C (3.5°F) and vast areas such as Dartmoor, which had been arable for thousands of years, had to be abandoned. Cultivation moved down towards heavier, more fertile, still forested slopes. The use of iron-tipped ploughs allowed many of the heavy wildland soils to be cultivated and during this remarkable period of agriculture it is probable that all areas of reasonable soil were cleared and ploughed. 'Home' woodlands of ash, hazel and wych elm were managed and coppiced to provide domestic items, agricultural utensils and, particularly, fuel. Wetlands were exploited for reed, sedge and peat. By the fifth century BC the landscape of the chalklands was already well farmed. Farmsteads were surrounded by a patchwork of squarish arable fields with, above them, open downlands for sheep. Below were larger woods, carefully managed by coppicing and, below them again on the rich valley floor, cereals and hay were cultivated to feed the stock in winter.

The Romans with their improved techniques probably farmed on a larger scale; and it was during the Roman occupation from the first to the fifth centuries AD, when the silt-rich floor of the Wash was emerging from the sea, that farmers enclosed the washlands – what we now call 'fen' – with sea banks and reclaimed them for agriculture. Nevertheless, much forest and wetland remained uncleared and undrained. After the decline of Rome many fields fell into disuse and scrub and woodland developed – parts of Hampshire, Dorset and Wiltshire have surviving ancient woodlands from this period.

A Saxon culture slowly emerged with groups of thatch and timber huts becoming hamlets.

People worked the land together on an infield-outfield system. The infield was an intensively coppiced area where all available manure was spread; the rougher outfield beyond it was grazed and possibly cultivated, with rest periods.

Further inroads were made into existing forest until the primary woodlands remained only in isolated blocks between either cultivated or ploughed fields. By the eleventh century woodland covered possibly only 15 per cent of Britain –

The rounded hills above this valley in Wales indicate glacial action. Open grazed moorland gradually gives way to

hedged fields and in the foreground is emergent scrubland of bracken with gorse.

twice the amount we have today. Hazel was the universal fuel and craft tree, with younger wood used for wattle work and faggots for burning, heating ovens, etc. Particular species were used for special purposes: ash for wagons and gates, beech for furniture, maple for domestic items like bowls, and alder or ash for hop poles.

Deep-seated changes had begun in the ninth century when woodland areas were cleared and ploughed particularly in the Weald. Earlier, settlements high on the exhausted chalkland were gradually deserted and new hamlets appeared on the edges of river valley flood plains. In central England village townships grew among open, unhedged fields – the country had few hedges or trees except in established and surviving woodland areas. Pasture woodlands developed during the eleventh century, after the Norman Conquest, when rights to rough graze the wastes of the manor were granted. In medieval times pasture under woodland was much more widespread; besides being found in wooded commons, it formed great tracts of royal forest. The system dominated much of central England then later spread north until, in modified form, it reached Scotland.

By the fourteenth century forest clearances were mainly of lowland areas as early medieval manorial fields and feudal holdings ate into the ancient woodlands and wastes. This continuing process was cut short in 1349 by the Black Death, the plague epidemic that killed between two-fifths and one-third of Europe's population. As a result of this death toll there was far more land than was necessary. Fields were abandoned around whole dead villages and much previously cul-

tivated land returned to woodland again. The yeoman farmer also emerged. Originally a labourer, he could build up capital from the increased wages that were paid to him because of the manpower shortage and, with this wealth, he could afford to buy farmland as a total package rather than a collection of strips – and might enclose this with hedges or stone walls.

Enclosure crept on during the centuries that followed and in the eighteenth and nineteenth centuries Enclosure by Act affected at least 3000 English parishes. By 1860 nearly half of England was enclosed as private property. Occasionally, where wooded commons were destroyed, oak and ash were planted in hedges to provide further timber. This period of enclosure enforced the rectilinear field pattern of much of our Midland landscapes, served by straight walls, hedges, fences and watercourses.

During the Industrial Revolution new coppices were planted in some areas where woods were few, such as in the north Midlands where there was a demand for charcoal for iron smelting and tanning. However, coppicing declined from the eighteenth century as alternative fuels became accessible and many coppices were cleared and replanted as high forest. Others were changed by the promotion of saplings to become later plantings of well-spaced oaks among coppice stools. Until recently these coppices with standard woodlands were being felled and cleared for farming.

So what we have today is a landscape patchwork, a combination of closed woodland of varying ages and open ground which might have been heath or moorland, pasture or downland, common land or arable ground or a form of wetland. And surrounding this are our coastal landscapes.

To relate this broad regional picture of differing landscapes to the scale of the average home and garden owner is difficult – and perhaps the best way is first to hone in on the individual environments and how they developed.

Beech woodland, traditionally grown for furniture making, with an understorey of holly. The foreground ditch is indicative of a previous boundary. Little grows beneath the beeches because of their solid leaf canopy and drip. Bluebells thrive in the well-drained soil beeches require, before the overhead foliage appears.

HEATHLAND AND MOORLAND

It is sobering to realize that most of what is now heath and moorland was once forested with pine, birch and oak. From pollen samples it has been deduced that early man cleared woodland on moderately deep, well-formed soil to make clearings. At first the soil was fertile, but once the woodlands were cleared they were probably cultivated, then used for pasture, and slowly their nutrients drained away. On the lowlands where the underlying rock was acidic poor acid soil that supported only heathland developed. On higher ground, and with more rain, infertile soils became moorland based on peat.

Bell heather, ling, heath, gorse or bracken and fine, acid-loving grasses with silver birch and some pine are typical of moorland and heathland.

This Peak District moorland of Derbyshire was once totally forested. Generations working the landscape deforested it for various forms of agriculture, though the foreground tussock grass does not indicate its use for more than grazing. New plantations of ubiquitous conifers now clothe the landscape. Large, walled moorland fields give way to smaller domestic ones towards the valley floor.

GRASSLANDS

The way in which native forest was cleared depended on physical conditions and their management, but as a generalization the most fertile soils, especially if they were rich in lime, were developed as grassland. There are very few places where grasslands are the norm. Scrub naturally takes over, working towards a climax vegetation of woodland, and many grasses disappear if they are not grazed or cut because coarser species oust them. Grasslands, or the open spaces between natural woodland, therefore have to be maintained against constant invasion. They are of various traditional types: downland, the hay meadow, the water meadow and common land. According to its management, each has developed its own vegetation – which is now disappearing fast as a result of twentieth-century cultivation techniques.

Downland is pasture on chalk or limestone hillsides and is rich in special flowers and butterflies. It developed from the first sheep-grazed areas during the sixteenth to nineteenth centuries. Seldom hedged, it is now broken up by fences. On chalk downland many native plants have foregone the race for light, which would expose them to the destruction of grazing rabbits and sheep, and have developed scattered rosettes bearing a profusion of flowers which fill the summer air with their herbal fragrance.

Vegetation typical of chalkland includes yew, whitebeam and box, the common rock rose, ox-eye daisy and woodbine.

While water was drained in East Anglia, it was introduced into flat chalkland areas in the eighteenth century to create the irrigated water meadows that still stripe the valley floors of Dorset, Hampshire and Wiltshire. Vast flocks of sheep grazed these meadows and then manured the arable land created by enclosing ancient downland pastures. Among the plants to be found in water meadows are marsh marigolds, the yellow iris and water forget-me-nots.

Hay meadows are often ancient and unimproved and therefore contain a wealth of wild flowers like meadowsweet, harebells, buttercups and cranesbill. They grow more slowly than modern 'improved' swards and are cut as late as July. Hay meadows may be opened up to stock after the hay crop and may be grazed until the autumn.

The vegetation of common lands varies as widely as the vegetation of Britain itself. Even now there are over 400 000 hectares (988 000 acres) of common land in England and Wales. These include huge areas of upland, most of it moorland, and some grassland where the soil is lime-rich and wild flowers abundant. The Lake District, Dartmoor, the Quantocks, the Cheviots and many of the Welsh hills are all areas of common land.

Rich grasslands, which for generations were only grazed, developed a fine tapestry of wild flowers. The necessity for higher productivity and use of chemical feeds altered this association for good – if they were not ploughed for arable usage. This field in the Midlands is of buttercups, with wild or cow parsley (*Anthriscus sylvestris*) in the hedgerow of elder (*Sambucus nigra*).

WETLAND

Wherever water has collected to form swamps and marshes, peat bogs and fens, special plant relationships, specific to individual locations, form and eco-systems develop.

Most wetland remaining in Britain is on the uplands of the north and west, the area that receives most rainfall and where glacial action caused topographic hollows in which water collects. The wetland areas of the lowlands are where flat country arrests the flow of a river and encourages the formation of oxbow lakes. This occurs particularly near estuaries. The fens, the Broads, the Somerset Levels, Romney Marsh and the smaller coastal waters of Pevensey, the Lancashire coast and Humber have all developed in this way.

Swamps, which may dry out in summer, are covered by grasses, sedges and rushes. Peat bogs may occur on elevated land, or in low-lying ground where the underlying rock is impervious. They support sedges, heather and bilberry.

Marsh is the transition from bog to dry land. Where it begins to dry out it supports grasses and herbs, followed by willow, birch and alder. Ultimately, such ground might support damp oakwoods.

Fens are marshy or artificially drained. Depending on the depth of the water, vegetation may be reedswamp, succeeded by white or crack willow, alder, buckthorn and bog myrtle. Guelder rose follows, with hawthorn.

The other large form of bog, the acid blanket bog, covers huge areas of high-altitude land with high rainfall and impeded drainage, such as western and Highland Scotland, Ireland, the Pennines and the Dartmoor plateau.

There are various forms of wetland, in varying stages of development from open water through bog, swamp or marsh. They can be freshwater or saltwater and are usually very rich in flora and fauna. Many areas of freshwater wetland have been drained for agriculture and development; much more is threatened.

In early spring reeds and rushes contrast with water lily (*Nymphae lutea*) pads and with white willow (*Salix alba*) and hawthorn (*Crateagus*) beyond.

VALLEYS AND RIVERS

Soils in these locations are transitions between waterlogged and drier types. They occur where the water table is variable between summer and winter and the ground may be alternately drained or waterlogged. They support ash and hazel, maple and wych elm and alder.

Above: Water descending over slate in an impoverished Welsh moorland landscape. The same slate is used for the boundary wall on the right. The foreground shrub is a native grey willow (*Salix cinerea*).

Right: The gentle meander of a Midland river through the rich earth of the valley floor. Over generations the river will alter its course through the valley as there is seldom rock to contain it.

COASTLAND

The last of the different habitats of plant association can be called coastland. Britain's coastline is one of the longest, richest and most varied in Europe and is still developing from its geological origins.

The habitats of its rocky coasts have changed little through history, but soft coastlines have seen perpetual changes created both by the sea and by man's attempts to gain ground for agriculture and industry. These have affected the vegetation enormously.

Coastal plants can be broadly divided into

three types. The first, the great majority, also live in other locations but occur near the coast because the unfarmed coastline provides an undisturbed corridor of heath or grassland, and sometimes woodland.

Prickly saltwort and sea rocket are examples from this category.

Plants in the second group live on the coast because it gives them a special ecological bonus

Above: Marram grass stabilizing sand-dunes. No other plant is able to grow both along the ground and vertically through blown sand, which it actually needs to thrive.

Above: Needles of a sedimentary rock jut into the sea. The sheltering grazed coastline is a mass of sea thrift and sea pink, followed by foxgloves and invasive bracken.

of some kind: shelter from frost, perhaps. Thrift, for instance, common on cliff tops, can tolerate some grazing but needs an open habitat, as does sea campion.

The third group is quite small. It consists of plants like marram and sand couch that can succeed with only a little water – growing in sand-dunes, perhaps – and are able to withstand strong wind and salt spray.

OUR NATIVE WOODLANDS

All Britain's regions were once surrounded, or covered, by woodland and the simplest way for the gardener to select the plants that are native to his region is to consider the trees that grow in his or her area. The layers or horizons of the different plant forms – wild flowers through shrubs – that are broadly characteristic of each region are defined by the types of woodland or climax vegetation with which they were or are associated. And it is within one of these regional areas that we all garden.

Ash and hazel, two of our most widespread trees, grow everywhere but on the most acid soils.

The English elm, much depleted by Dutch Elm disease in recent years is still just in evidence. But the smaller and older wych elm is more widespread. The commonest elm of ancient woods, it prefers deep moist soils, and occurs from the Mendips up through the Welsh borders. It also grows in lime-rich clays of the Midlands. Elm is also happy at the base of slopes, flushed with nutrient from above, and occurs in stands from Cornwall to the Scottish Highlands at the lower edges of upland oak and birch stands.

In the south-east, ash and wych elm stands are found on heavy clays and on lighter soils in East Anglia and Lincolnshire. Oak, which is different to pure oakwood vegetation, might have been planted into any of these permutations of woodland in the nineteenth century.

Pure oakwoods are confined to sites too acid or too starved for ash, maple or wych elm. Birch is part of the oakwood community and may

The male fern (*Dryopteris filix-mas*) growing among bluebells (*Scilla non-scripta*) in the light shade of a young oakwood.

survive and colonize after the oak has been cut. Oak and birch woodland varies from that of the lowland acid soils from Kent to Dorset to the sessile oakwoods of northern uplands. These oakwoods have an affinity to highland birch and rowan woods which become thinner at higher altitudes. Communities blend and change with soil types and altitude.

Beech is thought of as a tree of chalk, growing well on calcareous soils. In fact, it does well on acid clays and gravelly soils provided drainage is good. Most beechwoods are plantations, estab-lished after the Enclosure Acts of the nineteenth century for decorative purposes or to provide timber for furniture-making.

Alder woodland occurs where there is running, not stagnant, water. It prefers streamsides or the organic, peaty ooze of abandoned meanders.

Hornbeam was one of the last trees to arrive in Britain and is still more or less limited to areas in the south-east of the country. It forms stands on strongly acid soils with beech and hazel, or on heavy, wet clays with ash and maple.

Pine and birch were among the earliest trees

Left: Neglected oak woodland, where ivy begins to overcome any young growths the trees put out.

Right: The native primrose (*Primula vulgaris*) growing with sweet violet (*Viola odorata*).

Below: A coppiced woodland stand of sweet chestnut (*Castanea sativa*).

to colonize Britain as the ice retreated, but were replaced by larger-leaved species. Pine retreated to Scotland, while birch remained widespread as a subsidiary tree of lowland woods. True native ancient birchwoods are confined to upland sites, mainly in Scotland, on sites too poor to support other tree species except juniper, rowan or aspen. Pine on heathlands in southern Britain is probably of no great age – it was not reintroduced in the south until the mid-eighteenth century.

In the natural course of events, any of these forms of woodland provides a climax canopy, replacing scrub and cleared grassland. In our highly managed landscape, however, man has often retained or provided scrub and small trees for his own purposes. Species like hawthorn and blackthorn feature prominently in the patchwork of our fields – partly because they are tolerant of all manner of soils, but also because they are useful in hedges to keep cattle and sheep from wandering. To these may be added the bird cherry, the crab apple, elder, holly, spindle, the wayfaring tree, the wild cherry and the willow. Many of these native species occur in hedgerows.

OUR HEDGEROWS

As agriculture 'improved' fields were made larger to accommodate larger machinery. When hedges became a nuisance they were grubbed up. As a result, our landscape has undergone extensive reshaping. In the 1950s there was over 563 300 km. (350 000 miles) of hedgerow in Britain, but since then hedges have all but disappeared in some parts of the country, especially in East Anglia. In counties like Devon, which is not so suited to arable farming, traditional stock-rearing with smaller fields and therefore hedgerows persists.

The age of a hedgerow can be estimated from the average number of shrub species found in a 27 m (90 ft) stretch. The newest hedges were planted in the eighteenth and nineteenth centuries during the Enclosure Acts and usually contain hawthorn, the species favoured for its rapid growth and because of its thorny branches which deter animals from straying. Every additional shrub species in a hedge means that it is probably a further 100 years old.

Below: This hedge has been well laid – a task that can only be done by hand – and will regenerate fully clothed to the ground.

Below right: This roadside hawthorn (*Crataegus*) hedge has been flayed by a mechanical hedge trimmer. No attention was paid to its thinning base, no habitat has been provided for the local fauna, and lambs and calves could escape through the gaps in its base.

Left: The tapestry of this richly mixed hedge at the edge of woodlands is made up of wayfaring tree (*Viburnum lantana*), blackthorn (*Prunus spinosa*) and wild privet (*Ligustrum vulgare*) with oak behind. Wild flowers nestle in the base of the hedge providing an ideal habitat.

Below: In a 27 m (90 ft) run of hedge, the number of woody shrub or tree types, excluding woody climbers like blackberry (*Rubus fruticosus*), ivy (*Hedera helix*) and honeysuckle (*Lonicera periclymenum*), is indicative of the number of centuries for which it has been planted. The hedge in the diagram might be up to 500 years old.

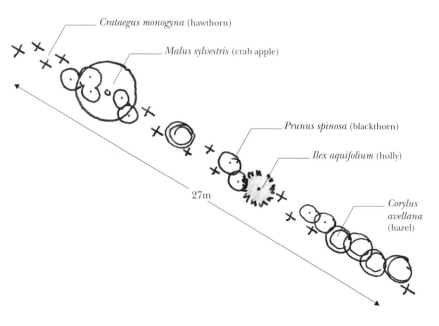

Crataegus monogyna (hawthorn)

Malus sylvestris (crab apple)

Prunus spinosa (blackthorn)

Ilex aquifolium (holly)

Corylus avellana (hazel)

27m

BORN FROM ITS ENVIRONMENT: THE COTTAGE GARDEN

In its purest form the cottage garden is the ultimate example of plants in their natural places. Traditionally, it was a garden of its setting, locked into its environment and tended by people who were in tune with the rhythms of nature. These early gardeners worked within the landscape that surrounded them – downland, forest or fen – and their gardens became a refined synthesis of what happened naturally, combining fruit with herbs and cultivated vegetables and with wild flowers from the hedgerows that surrounded and protected their plots.

The contemporary cottage garden in spring contains many more decorative subjects than its traditional ancestor.

THE TRADITIONAL COTTAGE GARDEN

Cottage gardens were probably inspired by the gardens of monastic houses where monks and nuns grew herbs for their healing properties and supplemented them with vegetables, salads and fruit to feed their communities. Such collections of plants developed inevitably into flower gardens, for many of the specimens that were taken from the wild and grown for their medicinal properties bore flowers and were valued as much for their scent as for their therapeutic qualities: the fragrance of violets, marjoram, pinks or primroses mixed with hay and strewn on the floor was a necessity in damp and badly ventilated buildings. Lilies and roses were valued for their religious significance as symbols of chastity and Christian love as well as for their perfume. Bulbs were crushed and used as salves and ointments.

The monastic garden was probably first copied by townspeople, for it was in towns that there first emerged a class of man who was free and who, without being rich, owned his own small house. Perhaps a craftsman or tradesman, he was protected by his guild from the great land-owning barons of the countryside. And it was in the town rather than the country, which provided its inhabitants with herbs and even wild vegetables, that it was necessary to cultivate pot herbs and salads. Furthermore, there was a market for this produce in the town; demand called supply into existence.

Before the Black Death in 1349 most people rented strips of land from the lord of the manor in return for working his land on certain days and paying him a proportion of their crops. But there was a scarcity of labour after the plague. Crops were neither sown nor harvested and labourers demanded high wages for their work. Landlords were forced to let their lands to tenants, and countrymen, increasingly independent of

Bayleaf, an oak-framed Wealden farmhouse of the sixteenth century, has been relocated amidst Sussex downland, at the Singleton Weald and Downland Museum. The setting is superb, surrounded by traditional woven hazel fencing that retains stock in a home meadow beneath beech trees.

their overlords, were able to build cottages for their families. With the appearance of the cottager in the English landscape and social system, the cottage garden emerged as well.

It is something of a paradox that when countrymen working the land began to have gardens they copied those of the townsman. A small and

usually rectangular plot, partially shaded by one or two apple trees, became the cottage garden norm. In the layout was a mixture of fragrant herbs and flowers taken from the wild, currant and gooseberry bushes and perhaps some wild strawberries. This part of the garden was an extension of nature; uncultivated, it was constantly enriched by the decay of fallen foliage. Elsewhere the cottager grew cabbages, broad beans, leeks and onions. And with them the primrose, cowslip and oxslip, with verbascum, hypericum and mallow from the wild. By the end of the fifteenth century the cottage garden 'form' had crystallized into a wild garden or 'flowery mead' with, nearby, an accompanying garden of herbs, salads and one or two vegetables, all partially shaded by fruit trees.

The plantings of such a garden were purely utilitarian. Food plants predominated and ornamentals were included only if they could be used medically: violets to relieve congestion, marigolds

for their anti-fungal properties and borage for 'loosening the bowels' are examples.

The larger part of the plot was given over to beans for flour and later there was a quarter-acre or half-acre of wheat, oats, barley or rye. It was a subsistence form of horticulture rather than a decorative one and a rotation of herbs and vegetables was vital to maintain good yields. This system was also used for field crops in agriculture, so the crop rotation of the garden often echoed the three-fold rotations in the fields that surrounded it.

A staple of the cottager's diet was the cabbage, referred to under a variety of names all of which

probably refer to the same kind of *brassica*. Cabbages, caul, kale, wortys or worts all formed the basis of a standard dish: the mess of potage, a vegetable stew with leeks, turnips and spinach.

Herbs were essential in this stew. They were also valued for their preservative, medicinal and digestive properties and were used to dye coarse fabrics, for crude beauty preparations and to flavour food. But the cottager probably valued them above all for their ability to ward off certain insects and plant diseases when they were grown next to specific plants: summer savory to keep beans free from aphids, parsley to deter carrot fly. This companion planting with its intercropping of herbs and vegetables created the glorious disorder of the traditional cottage garden.

Typically, a cottage garden was often part of

Left: Where space allowed the country cottager kept pigs, fowl and geese. These provided meat for the family – and valuable organic matter for the vegetable garden.

Right: In the cottage garden herbs are planted between rows of vegetables to ward off flies and insects. That the herbs flowered was incidental; such a garden would not have been considered ornamental in any way.

a larger farmstead and at Bayleaf, a Wealden farmhouse, there is a re-creation of just such a cottage garden of the mid-sixteenth century. Its owner at that time was probably a prosperous yeoman farmer who would have farmed as much as 40 hectares (100 acres). He may well have operated a nearby mill and also been involved in other commercial activities such as tanning or weaving. A community would have grown up around the farm.

The maintenance of the garden was the responsibility of the housewife, who could place her children in the safety of the fenced herber while she worked the garden. A farmworker

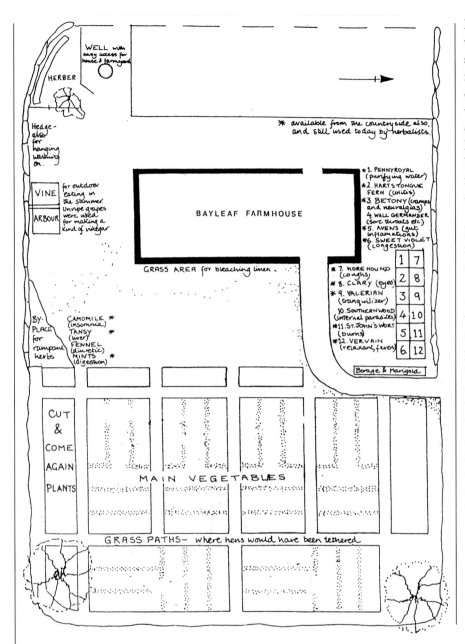

WELL with easy access for house & farmyard

HERBER

Hedge- also for hanging washing on.

VINE — for outdoor eating in the summer. Unripe grapes were used for making a kind of vinegar

ARBOUR

BY- PLACE for rampant herbs

CAMOMILE * (insomnia)
TANSY * (liver)
FENNEL (diuretic)
MINTS (digestion) *

* available from the countryside also, and still used today by herbalists.

BAYLEAF FARMHOUSE

GRASS AREA for bleaching linen.

*1. PENNYROYAL (purifying water)
*2. HARTS TONGUE FERN (colitis)
*3. BETONY (cramps and neuralgias)
4. WALL GERMANDER (sore throats etc)
*5. AVENS (gut inflamations)
*6. SWEET VIOLET (congestion)

*7. HOREHOUND (coughs)
*8. CLARY (eyes)
*9. VALERIAN (tranquilizer)
10. SOUTHERNWOOD (internal parasites)
*11. ST. JOHN'S WORT (burns)
*12. VERVAIN (relaxant, fevers)

1	7
2	8
3	9
4	10
5	11
6	12

Borage & Marigold

CUT & COME AGAIN PLANTS

MAIN VEGETABLES

GRASS PATHS— where hens would have been tethered

Not an inch of ground was wasted around the sixteenth-century farmhouse. As this plan of Bayleaf shows, there was a place for everything. The pig was kept in a barn at the back of the house and fowl also strutted in his enclosure.

Medicinal and dyeing herbs were separated from those for companion planting.

Early rotations of crops were in three-yearly cycles and two separate cycles are possible in this garden. On one side of the central path is the main vegetable garden; the two vertical rectangular plots and the horizontal rectangle work as one cycle and this is repeated on the other side of the path.

helped with the heavy digging. When the housewife rested it would have been upon a turf seat within the herber.

As well as the house and garden, Bayleaf farmstead also included an orchard, barn and yard all of which bore little relationship to each other. A pig and some fowl were kept in the yard to provide meat and eggs. The small fields surrounding the farmstead were fenced with con-tinuous woven or wattled hazel, with panels of cleft hazel for smaller folds.

Shaws or thickets were planted in rows to give shelter to the farmstead and provide additional food and timber and were managed so that there was a row of timber trees down the middle with regularly coppiced shrubs forming a lower layer. The plantings included ash, oak, crab apple, field maple, laurel, hawthorn, holly, wild cherry and wild roses. The timber, coppiced poles, wild fruits and seeds were used within the farm community.

Over the generations, cottagers – whether they were prosperous like the owners of Bayleaf or more humble farmworkers – practised a measure of improved selection among the plants in their gardens, digging up a double primrose, propagating the colour variation in a violet, taking home from the wild a periwinkle, a native iris, a cranesbill, daffodil, foxglove, campion or monkshood.

Hazel, pear, apple and hawthorn were introduced into gardens, with honeysuckle and wild rose (*Rosa gallica*) creeping in of their own accord. In limestone neighbourhoods, yew and box

used for the house, wall or fence; whether the roof was tile, slate or thatch; and whether the surrounding landscape was hilly and open or flat and wooded.

There is little reason to suppose that either size, form or content altered much between the

Above: This plant (*Chenopodium album*) is called fat hen. An annual, it was used as a potherb and boiled and eaten like spinach. It might also have been part of the 'mess of potage' that was a staple of the householder's diet.

Left: The fences are of woven hazel to deter rabbits with, in front of them, three traditional bee skeps. The ground between the skeps might have contained wild flowers.

appeared with native viburnum; in acid-loving moorland areas heather and ling were used with broom.

Although cottage garden layouts became more compartmented and organized as crop rotation became commonplace, regional differences in soil and climate still made them look very different from each other. Their overall appearance was influenced by whether stone, brick or wood was

fifteenth and seventeenth centuries, for while fashions changed for the wealthier members of society they would have had little effect on the countryman. Father and brothers might work 'up at the manor' and might occasionally smuggle slips or cuttings of new 'introduced' plants back to the cottage, but on the whole there was little change: the cottage garden was essentially an economic necessity.

This plan prepared by the Weald and Downland Museum in West Sussex shows the cropping plan for only one season. Major beds would be rotated so that root crops and green crops did not grow in the same bed in sequential years.

Herbs are grown round the cropping beds but would have been interplanted as well.

This is intensive cultivation, which would have been carried out by the farmer's wife to provide a very basic diet for a probably enormous family. At the back of the house fowls were run along with the pigs. This was self-sufficiency in its truest form.

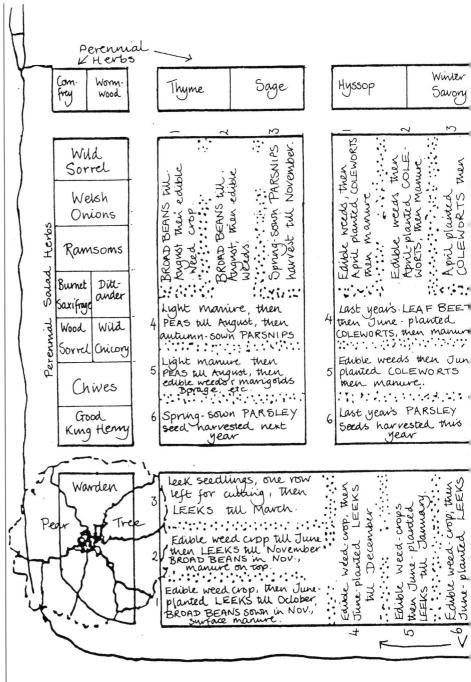

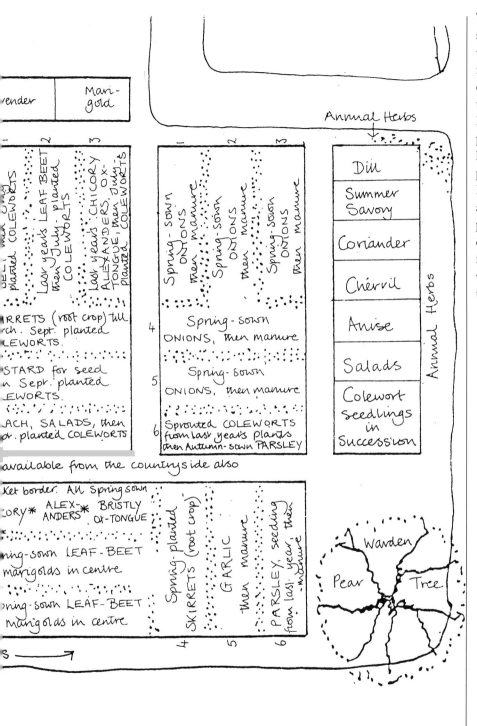

This cropping plan gives some idea of the kinds of vegetables and herbs that made up the typical diet of a cottager's family in the sixteenth century. Broad beans, peas, parsnips, leaf beet and leeks were the predominant vegetables. Edible wild plants were also a feature of the plantings and herbs like chicory were garnered from the countryside as well as being planted in the cottage garden.

Annual Herbs

Dill

Summer Savory

Coriander

Chérvil

Anise

Salads

Colewort Seedlings in Succession

Annual Herbs

...ender | Mari-gold

...ELL ...ed COLEWORTS

Last year's LEAF BEET 2 then July-planted COLEWORTS 3

Last year's CHICORY, ALEXANDERS, OX-TONGUE, then July-planted COLEWORTS

Spring-sown ONIONS then manure 2

Spring-sown ONIONS then manure 3

Spring-sown ONIONS then manure

...RRETS (root crop) till ...ch. Sept. planted ...LEWORTS.

...STARD for seed ...n Sept. planted ...EWORTS.

...ACH, SALADS, then ...t. planted COLEWORTS

4 Spring-sown ONIONS, then manure

5 Spring-sown ONIONS, then manure

6 Sprouted COLEWORTS from last year's plants then Autumn-sown PARSLEY

available from the countryside also

...ket border. All Spring sown ...ORY* ALEX-* BRISTLY ANDERS* OX-TONGUE

...ing-sown LEAF-BEET marigolds in centre

...ning-sown LEAF-BEET marigolds in centre

Spring-planted SKIRRETS (root crop) 4

GARLIC then manure 5

PARSLEY, seeding from last year, then manure 6

Warden Pear Tree

...S ➞

THE INDUSTRIAL COTTAGE GARDEN

The Industrial Revolution of the eighteenth century encouraged countrymen, particularly in the north of England, to leave the land to find work in towns and here their cottage gardens took the form of allotments, often some distance from their homes, where they grew vegetables. Those that remained in the country were increasingly affected by the Enclosure Acts which, during the eighteenth and nineteenth centuries, turned common ground into private property.

Some countrymen received smallholdings as a

Right: The back garden of Squatters' Cottage at Blists Hill – the nineteenth-century industrial version of the country cottage. Fowl run beneath a simple selection of fruit trees.

Below: A large family would be raised in a home like this, although there was only a small vegetable plot (combined with flowers) to feed its members.

result of the Acts, but many sold these for ready money and, as industry beckoned, the land returned to the big landowners. Others continued as farm labourers, though cottage and garden were now 'tied' and were lost if and when a worker was dismissed. Yet others were squatters – tenants of landlords in the country, towns or villages who were not granted land rights and who built their own dwellings.

Inevitably, the area of the cottage garden

became smaller, calling for a greater rationalization of the remaining land to feed an all-too-often hungry family.

At Blists Hill, which is part of the Ironbridge Gorge Museum, a cottage has been built and furnished to show exactly how squatters might have lived in an industrial valley of the Severn Gorge in the 1890s.

In the nineteenth century Blists Hill was part of an important coal-mining area and it is in

Squatters Cottage that a miner, his wife and his often large family lived. Adjacent to the cottage there is a small garden. The planting is mainly herbs and some flowers like chrysanthemums – a favourite – dahlias and spring bulbs, and is fenced to keep out the fowl that run free in the garden. Like their predecessors, these later cottagers also kept a pig.

Below the cottage there is a small paddock with grazing for the goats that provided milk and possibly a donkey, the family's main means of transport. As water was available ducks and geese would also have run in the pasture.

Like the owners of Bayleaf, the tenants of Squatters Cottage had to live off their land as far as possible; and although the garden at Blists Hill is a later, more urbanized version of the one in the Weald its functions have hardly changed. For the real cottage garden is a countryman's smallholding.

THE DESIGNED COTTAGE GARDEN

Although the traditional cottage garden has never vanished completely, more recent versions lack the spontaneity of the originals. Their romantic effect is achieved more by design than artlessness. For in the mid-nineteenth century gardening began to become a hobby for an emergent middle class and was concerned with control, maintenance and the eradication of the 'weed'. It was also the period when introduced and improved forms of plant became the criteria of the content of the garden.

Paradoxically enough, just when the artificiality of the typical Victorian garden had reached the heights of fashion, leaders of the Romantic movement were looking back to the land and its native plants. They were the inheritors of the vogue for 'the beautiful wilderness' that had its roots in seventeenth-century concepts of nature and wildness and the gardens created by Capability Brown in the eighteenth century and Humphrey Repton. However, this English school of landscape design was too perfect – indeed its practitioners were known as 'the improvers' who ironed out the crudenesses of raw nature – and by the late nineteenth century the romantic approach, coupled with the Arts and Crafts movement, had led to a renewed appreciation of the cottage garden as it really had been with its muddle of unsophisticated plant material. This more realistic approach was led by the writer William Robinson who, in 1883, wrote one of the most influential of all gardening books: *The English Flower Garden*. In it he praises the simplicity of the cottage garden and finds the secret of its charm in the absence of any pretentious plan.

Sixteen years after the publication of *The English Flower Garden* Gertrude Jekyll brought out *Wood and Garden*, her first book. In this and her many subsequent writings she calls on her insight into the cottage garden, which she researched thoroughly in rural Surrey, and on her considerable knowledge of the natural forms and plant groupings that grew from its landscape.

Time and again she pays tribute to cottage gardens, for: 'They have a single and tender charm that many look for in vain in gardens of grander pretensions.

'And the old garden flowers,' she adds, 'seem to know that there they are seen at their best.'

Gertrude Jekyll was unique. In her plantings, particularly those for Sir Edwin Lutyens' country house gardens, she managed to weld grand and humble concepts together and led both away from the ideals of the Victorian garden. And although the maintenance of the type of garden which her clients owned is well beyond today's average gardener, the romantic mood of her gardens still pervades the English country garden scene.

It is the 'essence' of her approach to plant associations – her concern for colour gradation as well as textural quality and scale in her plant masses – which seems to engage us still. For unique in the world, the English gardener still maintains his or her hands-on approach to plants and their arrangement, a persistent thread which links us through Gertrude Jekyll back to earlier, earthier origins on the land.

The tradition of the cottage garden has influenced not only the plant material but the walling in this garden of 'grander pretensions' – to quote Miss Jekyll. The yellow spires are of our native mullein (*Verbascum thapsus*), deliciously drifted as they might grow in the wild.

A COTTAGE GARDEN TODAY

The cottage garden as we know it is very much a seasonal garden. Winter has a bleak, brown charm punctuated with stems and bark against dark yew, though if you look closer you will see that by New Year aconites, snowdrops and winter hellebores have replaced ferns and holly berries as the stars. From then until the flush of spring there is a growing crescendo of interest with dog's mercury in the wood and winter heliotrope in boggy ditches. In the west, the early primrose appears under hazel catkins and pussy willow. Follow this with bluebell sheets beneath early woodland leaves, and coltsfoot and buttercup in worked ground. As leafy shade forms a darkening canopy, flowers leave the woodland and move to open ground on banks and roadsides, to meadows (untreated by man) and to the waterside. By early summer, many of our wild flowers are spent and the interest moves to hedgerows with wild roses, brambles and honeysuckle. Grasses grow tall and flower to accompany autumn shades as flowers fade and berries take over.

Native plant interest is cyclical and while introduced plant material can supplement it, it should not swamp it. Strong introduced foliaged forms or variegations or alien colour mixes disturb the natural look, particularly when they are seen against a landscape view.

The garden of Addisford Cottage is a twentieth-century example of a cottage garden in total harmony with its surroundings. The house, built

The garden of this West Country cottage is basically a clearing in a wood. The profusion of flowers and plant forms epitomizes the languor of summer days and the supposed charm of a bygone era. This lovely mixture is a twentieth-century version of a traditional cottage garden for many of the plants are imported. The interest is that they are grown in a 'country' way.

of cob and thatch, stands in an isolated but sheltered West Country valley amidst neatly hedged fields and ferny oakwoods. It is perhaps two or three hundred years old.

The cottage was originally part of an estate and would have been the home of a farmworker and his family. Its situation near a stream would have provided water for washing, drinking and sanitation. Within living memory, what is now garden grew only vegetables. There was nothing decorative in sight and fowl ranged freely on the hill behind the cottage. This was the reality of country living, even in the twentieth century.

The cottage is approached across a ford. The stream continues to serpentine round the garden on its northern border and the view from the house is south across the garden to the wooded streamside and the flower meadow and woods beyond it. Left and right of the main view the garden fades into woodland. Originally oak with coppiced hazel (which would have been used to 'stitch' the thatch and provide stakes), it now,

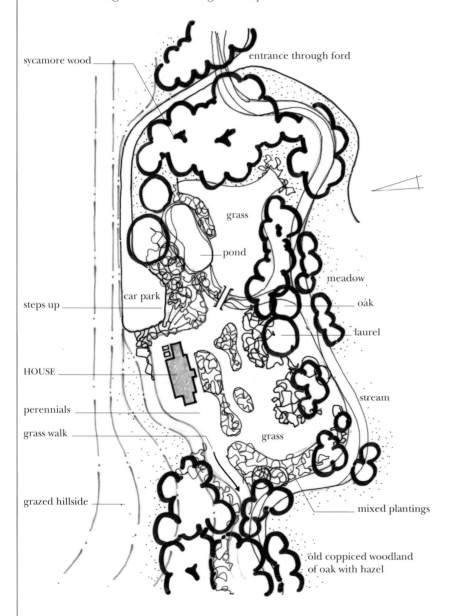

sycamore wood

entrance through ford

grass

pond

meadow

car park

oak

steps up

laurel

HOUSE

stream

perennials

grass walk

grass

grazed hillside

mixed plantings

old coppiced woodland
of oak with hazel

Right: The drawback to a total flower garden lacking obvious evergreen bones is its thinness in winter. Actually there are aconites, snowdrops, hellebores and *Iris foetidissima* beneath the trees giving incidental interest.

Left: The entrance to Addisford Cottage is across a ford shown at the top of the plan. A drive leads to the house. The garden, to the south of the cottage, is bordered by a stream. Beyond the garden to the west is the old coppiced woodland. A hillside runs up behind the house, protecting it from the north.

At the edge of the garden decorative subjects can blend with native ones provided the scale of their numbers is in scale with the wider view outside. Bleeding heart (*Dicentra formosa*) is here drifted with a cultivated form of our native cranesbill (*Geranium sanguineum*). The fern is invasive bracken, not to be encouraged.

Some areas are acid where the ground has been worked and others are shale and quite alkaline. The highest part, where the cottage is set into a shaley bank, is grey clay with deep loam by the stream bed.

The sheltered valley is a frost pocket. The garden is late in getting the sun even in summer and because it is behind the trees of the surrounding woodland, never sees the setting sun. Even on such a south-facing plot, trees have to be constantly pruned back to let in as much sunlight as possible. They grow like mad with the combination of shelter and West Country rain. The multi-stemmed effect of the hazels and alders makes it very obvious that this process has gone on for generations, and the present owners are all too aware of holding the very considerable forces of nature constantly in check.

This seemingly idyllic spot is therefore not an easy one in which to garden. Soil variation, damp, shade and limited sun all affect the selection of suitable decorative plant material. Where there is sunlight, and against the shelter of the cottage, it is possible to grow a good range of perennial – even exotic – material. But further away from the house, anything coniferous other than native box, yew or holly, looks wrong. Variegated or gold foliages seem very alien. The owners have been trying shrub roses with suitable perennials and grasses, but many are subject to black spot.

Despite all these problems, after only six years the garden looks superb in summer. Paths lead the eye through trees to woodland beyond and the foreground planting is a lovely hug-a-mug of this and that – there is no sophisticated colour-ranging here. This is what Gertrude Jekyll was writing about: the garden as an expression of its surroundings. It even looks bright in the short, dark days of damp December, with gleaming ferns underfoot, white honesty seed heads penetrating the dark red plates of sedum masses – and the first, pale primrose flowers with a mass of shooting snowdrop bulbs.

inevitably, includes sycamore. Underfoot in spring are primroses with an ivy ground cover through which bluebells grow. In the damper, lower part of the garden beneath fast-growing alders are banks of snowdrops which are followed in late spring by ramsons or wild garlic.

The soil changes considerably on the site.

PEOPLE AND PLANTS: AN UNEASY RELATIONSHIP

Most designed gardens of the nineteenth century, including those of Sir Edwin Lutyens which Gertrude Jekyll subsequently planted, were functional extensions of the house – outside 'rooms' or a series of rooms. Layouts tended to be classic. Main paths formed vistas and subsidiary paths at right angles to them defined space as a balanced symmetric progression from the house. The manner of their decoration and styling was also classic, with Roman balustrades, Tuscan pots and urns or Grecian temples.

The twentieth century has seen new design influences – an international style spearheaded by the architects and designers of the Modernist movement and, more recently, a return to 'natural' gardening.

The strong shape of
Modernist buildings is a good
foil for bold architectural
planting compositions.

MODERNISM AND THE INTERNATIONAL STYLE

Early in the twentieth century a group of designers in Austria and Germany reacted against the classical tradition. The Modernists, as they became known, felt that in a new industrialized age of mass-produced goods, when houses and furnishings utilized new materials and techniques, a more forward-looking lifestyle made sense. The frippery of the swag and the strait-jacket of the classic order had been superseded, they believed, by twentieth-century concepts in art, architecture and sculpture. Lines were to be cleaner, with a stronger emphasis on shape than colour.

Much of this early influence came from the interest in Japanese style. In Japan, houses were uncomplicated structures whose walls swept back to reveal stylized garden settings which were themselves supposed to represent a symbiosis of wild landscape. To achieve this effect plants were clipped and trained and rocks were used symbolically, set off by sheets of tranquil water or even raked sand. Seasonal colour effects swept through the garden at cherry time and iris time – a far cry from the English perennial border.

The Modernists were also influenced by new concepts of abstraction and symmetry. With the influence of painters such as Mondrian and Klee the public saw for the first time pattern and colour expressed on paper as a joy in itself. The purity of this school had developed slowly through Impressionism late in the nineteenth century then Cubism early in the twentieth. Subject matter was less and less important as line and balance, and then colour, became more significant.

Sculpture too moved from chill classic forms of the human torso through Rodin and then Matisse to the more abstract organic forms of Epstein and Moore.

In the 1930s, with the rise of Nazism, Modernism moved to the United States, leap-frogging

The shape of this swimming pool is inspired by the winding creeks of the salt marshes beyond the live oaks at its far end. Designed and built in the 1940s by Thomas Church at Sonoma near San Francisco, it stands out as a testimony to the validity of Modernism in garden design.

Britain whose tentative exploration of Modernist theory was brought to a halt by the Second World War. In America, under the leadership of Walter Gropius and then Mies van der Rohe, Modernism gave way to an International movement in architecture. Landscape designers started to explore new, simplified forms of organic shapes which fitted gardens into landscapes. Released

from the symmetry of the classic, the newer garden shapes followed the Modernist dictum that 'form follows function' to accommodate the swimming pool, the drive, the garage and the parking lot. All these influences are seen in the work of the late Thomas Church and James Rose and Garret Eckbo and Dan Kiley.

A further huge design influence came from Brazil during the late 1940s in the work of Roberto Burle Marx, who used broad masses of native plant material within organic patterning to create a scaled relationship between planting pattern, the form of the land and the surrounding landscape.

The architect Frank Lloyd Wright rejected the Modernist principle of form following function in

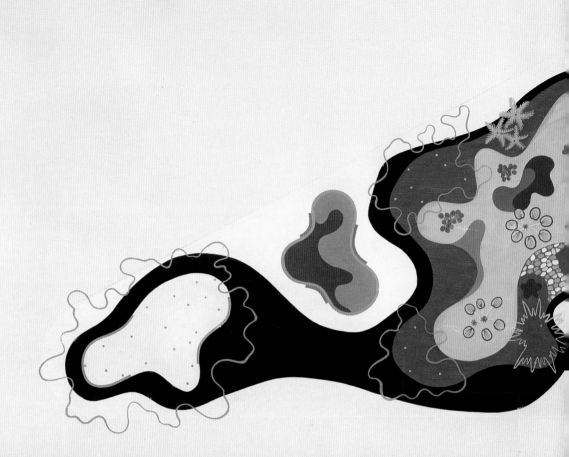

building and sought to evolve an architecture in an updated vernacular of the mid-West. Although the siting of his buildings was often superb, he was not interested in garden design and called upon his friend Jens Jensen, a Danish landscape designer who was passionately keen on the 'essence of place' and the use of native plant materials, to weld buildings into their sites – an interesting new development.

Although some of these new design theories began to make themselves felt in Britain early in the 1950s, with the Festival of Britain, their influence was at first limited. The public was

Above: The Brazilian landscape architect Roberto Burle Marx explored new areas of garden design with his bold organic shapes, incorporating sweeps of plant material as part of the overall design. He originally used native tropical plants to infill the

exciting patterns that related his gardens to the landscapes that surrounded them. Later, however, he hybridized much of this material; Burle Marx was a great plantsman as well as a twentieth-century designer of merit.

deterred by post-war Brutalist buildings based on the Modernist ideal. And our gardens, if we designed them at all, continued to be laid out in classic form; plantings were still in the mould of Gertrude Jekyll, whose organic message seemed far cosier.

Nevertheless, the Modernist movement's influence has slowly filtered through in Britain. And whether or not we like the buildings and artefacts it has produced is unimportant. Its theories on design are proven and enable us to produce new working plans or designs in which asymmetry is combined with the use of sympathetic building material. This does not deny the classic formal look. It too is proven; but will only be used where appropriate.

Right: This newly restored garden was strongly influenced by Cubist painting with its emphasis on geometric and inter-related shapes. It was designed in 1926 by Gabriel Guévrékian for a house by the Modernist architect Robert Mallet-Stevens at Hyères in France.

PLANTS AND PESTICIDES

Existing side by side with our garden layouts, even surrounding them, was an agriculture that was slowly eradicating our native plant material. To increase crop yields through the years of the world wars we had grown away from the traditional method of feeding the land with organic matter. Instead we relied more and more on inorganic feeds and chemical sprays to husband it. But by the 1960s there was a growing disillusionment with this excessive used of chemicals. In *Silent Spring*, published in 1962, Rachel Carson drew attention to an imbalance between efficient food production and the ecological balance of the countryside. Her attack was not on the use of chemicals in general, but on the indiscriminate use of some in particular, especially pesticides, which had the boomerang effect of wiping out natural predators or clearing the way for other, equally troublesome, pests. As farming became more specialized, so the land became more vulnerable to infestation.

The use of chemicals was by no means directed solely towards pests. Modern methods of cultivation demand a much wider array of chemicals, the least threatening perhaps being fertilizers. But fertilizers make weeds as well as cereals grow. So their application was accompanied by frequent sprays with herbicide to eradicate those weeds – many of which are commonly known to us as wild flowers.

These two illustrations show up the visual difference between older farming methods and a current 'weed-free' monoculture. The physical effects these different approaches have on the land and the wildlife it supports can only be appreciated with close examination. But a weed-free monoculture can be a killer since it allows for no diversity.

A meadow in Gloucestershire (left) has been farmed the old way and in it the gold of buttercups is mixed with grass and other perennial wild flowers.

A field of oil-seed rape in Oxfordshire (below left) has been subjected to more intensive farming methods and is much more strident visually and far more demanding in its maintenance.

THE WAY AHEAD

Today there is an increasing awareness of the need to conserve our native fauna and use our native flora, and a greater sympathy with the earth. Increasingly, pest control is being handled biotechnically, with genetically engineered substances eliminating pests and allowing pest-resistant strains of plant to be bred. But there is also a return to organics, to a new, organically based philosophy for husbanding the earth with a closer examination of eco-systems and the plant cycles and associations within them.

On the public scale there are now large, landscaped schemes based upon ecological principles, for pleasure parks, wetland areas and other recreational centres. Their subtlety is that they both serve their function and preserve the integrity of the landscape within which they are sited. These public areas are today's examples of good landscape design; there are few patrons to foster designed gardens on the scale of the past.

On the private scale, however, while the British have an undoubted feel for their landscapes, celebrated in music, painting and literature, and also have an undoubted feel for their gardens, the two seldom seem to come together.

As gardeners we remain curiously conservative. Many of our gardening techniques are still a reflection of a former affluent, country-house lifestyle in an ordered society, one in which even garden plants were obliged to conform to some regimented system. The tension existing between the wild and the cultivated is probably as old as man, and where nature was once overwhelming it is now struggling to survive. Yet we still seek to knock it into shape and subordinate what happens naturally.

And, rather than taking account of the mechanics of the ecology that sustains the look of our landscapes, we are happy to disturb our

Some of the most sensitive approaches to landscape are by visual artists who have the eye to see organic shapes and forms and who are able to analyse their surroundings and work with them.

Ian Hamilton Findlay is a poet and sculptor as well as a gardener. Sculpted incidents within his Scottish garden combine the past with the future in a way that is extraordinarily timeless – and natural for today.

This piece – 'Pan's Pipes' – carved in stone reads: 'When the winds blow venerate the sound.' The early spring planting around it is of the emergent leaves of meadowsweet with blue early forget-me-nots and, beyond, yellow-flowering leopard's bane.

countryside with domestic cultivation, the introduction of exotics and the excessive use of inorganic substances. It is a sobering thought that most suburban lawns receive a far higher concentration of chemicals than the typical farmer's field.

I believe the way ahead is to take a closer look at the garden within its setting, to study the natural plant associations which create that setting and to learn from them. Perhaps the gardens that come closest to this ideal are those of painters or sculptors who seek a broader picture and who live where they do because of its landscape. They do not seek to alter, 'improve' or suppress it. Rather, they seek to be of it.

Among these I would include Clyde Holmes on the bleak moorlands of North Wales and Ian Hamilton Findlay in Scotland. One uses his surroundings to paint, the other as a backdrop to his sculpture. On treeless Cornish cliffs the artist Patrick Heron has created a garden of Zen perfection with rock and moss and what will survive the winter winds.

On the south coast of Kent, the late Derek Jarman cultivated an extraordinary range of

The garden of the late Derek Jarman, a writer and film producer, was created on the shingle of the Kent coast. The saline-laden wind and absence of soil necessitated a limited range of plant material that was adapted to such hard conditions. Plants are small-leafed and tufted – and, being of their surround, are totally in tune with it.

plants, herbs and vegetables using them as decoratives in the true tradition of a cottage garden – but a garden growing out of a gravel beach and blasted by winds straight from Siberia. He used driftwood and pebble arrangements to integrate his design ideas with the wild through plantings of sea pink, sea crambe, mallow and tansy with wild broom and shrub roses.

On the Dorset coast the painter John Hubbard has created a sheltered, roomed garden for exotics, for he is a traditional plant collector. But the same eye has integrated outbuildings, fences and even a swimming pool beyond the garden walls into their wild, bold landscape of chalk downland and sheep.

In a way we have come full circle, for all regional cottage gardens were born of their landscapes. And today we should reinterpret their message. We must put aside romantic associations, analyse the real functions of the garden and, through a new awareness of design, relate these functions to our non-cottage homes and current lifestyles.

Above: The painter John Hubbard has a walled garden that is full of choice plant material, for he is a collector. But beyond an old cowshed, which has become the pool house, outside the garden, his swimming pool sits proudly in its Dorset landscape. The far side of the pool acts as a sort of ha-ha, so sheep are kept at bay.

Right: Tradition mixes here with a planter's eye. Topiary shapes of box and yew contrast with the vertical of the chimney. The picture is dominated by a fine group of grey artichoke leaves – quite refreshingly modern.

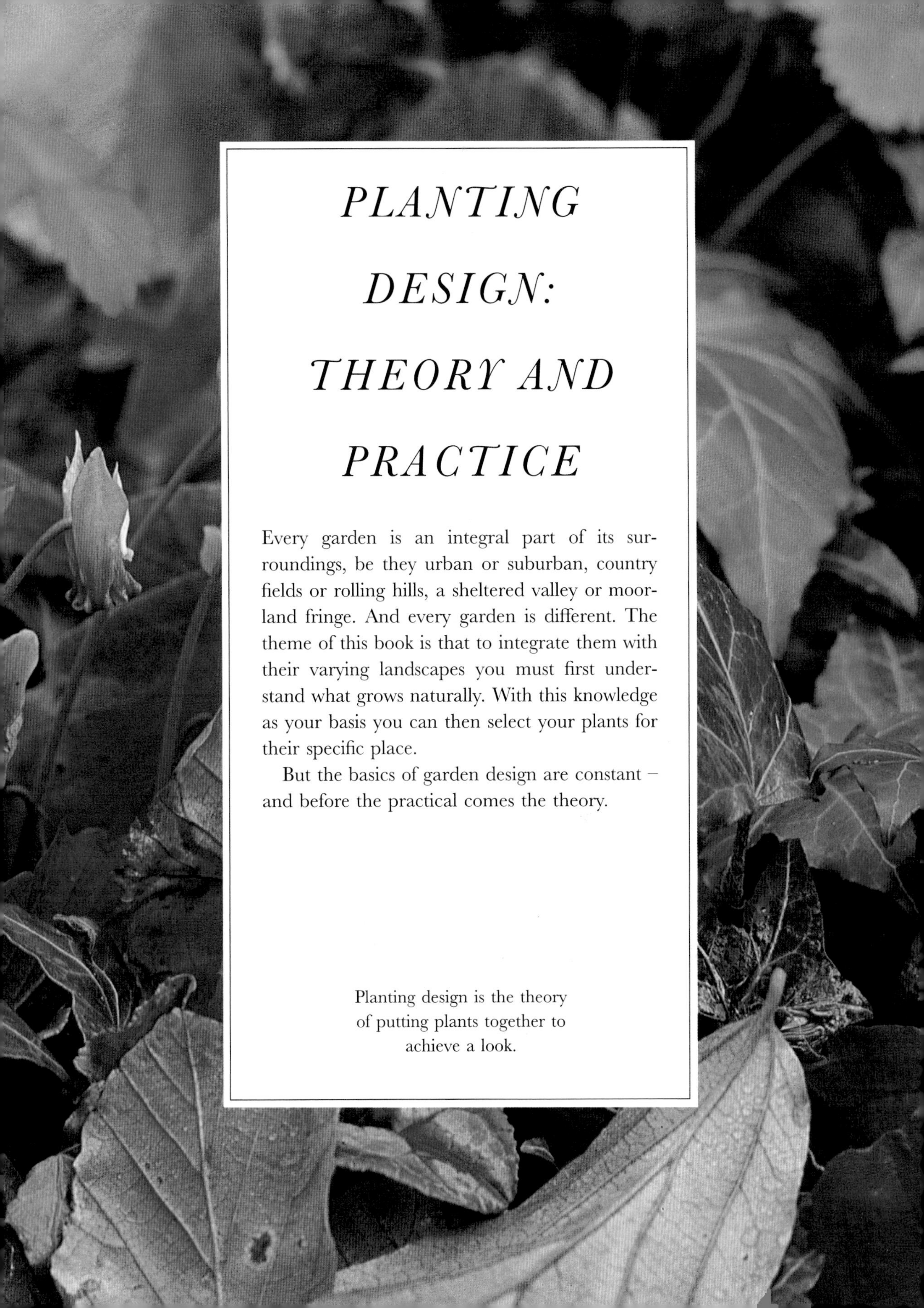

PLANTING DESIGN: THEORY AND PRACTICE

Every garden is an integral part of its surroundings, be they urban or suburban, country fields or rolling hills, a sheltered valley or moorland fringe. And every garden is different. The theme of this book is that to integrate them with their varying landscapes you must first understand what grows naturally. With this knowledge as your basis you can then select your plants for their specific place.

But the basics of garden design are constant – and before the practical comes the theory.

Planting design is the theory
of putting plants together to
achieve a look.

THE BASICS

Much of the theory of plant design will have to
be interpreted according to the scale of your
garden and the surroundings in which it sits.
Landscape need not be pastoral. It can be suburban and although your garden may be small
there could be 10 m (32 ft) or 15 m (50 ft) trees on
a railway line opposite the house or in the garden
next door. Even the back of a neighbour's garage
could be a visual element.

Whatever it is, it will affect the scale of the
planting you choose to accompany it. Although

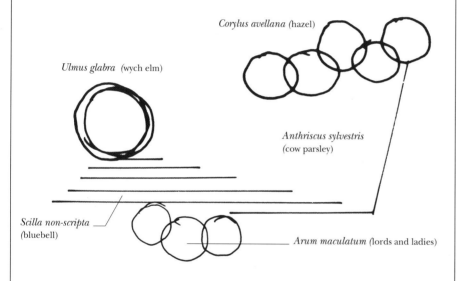

Corylus avellana (hazel)

Ulmus glabra (wych elm)

Anthriscus sylvestris
(cow parsley)

Scilla non-scripta
(bluebell)

Arum maculatum (lords and ladies)

you can deflect the eye and provide a rival
attraction instant hiding would be difficult. The
scale of your alternative should therefore be
considered in terms of peripheral objects.

On the other hand, you may identify a major
attraction – a tree or trees in your garden or a
distant view of the countryside. If you do, work
to that. The scale of your planting should also
relate to your house when you look back at it
from the bottom of the garden. This will couch
the building into its site with the vegetation

Above: Plan showing the
plants that frame the view
beyond the garden in the
illustration on the right.

Much can be learnt from this natural incident at the edge of a garden. First, the hedge of elm (*Ulmus glabra*) and hazel (*Corylus avellana*) frames a view to fields beyond. Bluebells (*Scilla non-scripta*) and cow parsley (*Anthriscus sylvestris*) merge together in a natural way. Lords and ladies (*Arum maculatum*) make a feature in the foreground. Mixed ferns follow in the dappled shade. Primroses (*Primula vulgaris*) under the hedge have faded before an overhead canopy of leaves emerges.

becoming the transition between the height of the vertical walls of the house and the breadth of the level garden.

You may have inherited a tree whose scale far outweighs that of the house and its surroundings so that nothing grows around it and you are in perpetual shade. Have absolutely no hesitation in felling it – provided, of course, that it is not covered by a preservation order. Check with your local planning office. Use a qualified and insured tree surgeon to do the job. As long as you are going on to plant other, more suitable, trees you need have no qualms whatsoever.

Because of our romantic attitude to trees many people, particularly in rural locations, allow themselves to be hemmed in and separated from the landscapes that surround them. Gardeners of earlier generations sought shelter and enclosure for their exotics, often at the expense of their views, and any subsequent neglect allows the trees they planted to grow out of scale. With careful thinning or felling your landscape can flow into your garden to be part of it. Your subsequent planting will be planned to further enhance the concept.

MASS AND VOID

The masses created by the heights of trees, the density of their plantings and the bulk of your house or neighbouring buildings are as important as their individual scales. How they contrast with the open spaces between them – the void – dictates whether or not you have a balanced garden planting and whether or not you feel comfortable in your garden. If the planted mass is too low and the void between the masses too great, you do not feel couched or sheltered. You can be said to be *on* rather than *in* your garden; you feel exposed. Alternatively, if houses are too close together you lack privacy and feel equally exposed. It is this yearning for visual shelter that has led to the ubiquitous planting of so much *Ch. leylandii.* As many know to their cost, they soon grow out of scale so that their bulky height is too great for the garden void at the base.

Much can be learnt about keeping plant material in scale by using earlier forms of coppicing native vegetation. Coppicing is a form of pruning where individual plants are selected on rotation to be cut down (not felled) so that none of them become too large.

Left: On a windswept rocky shoreline of the Solway Firth a natural grouping of wild flowers has drifted itself through a boulder bank. These perennials have self-seeded themselves to provide swathes of gentle colour. The grey-leafed poplar (*Populus canescens*) provides a wonderful backdrop linking the colour of the sky with the estuary's grey waters.

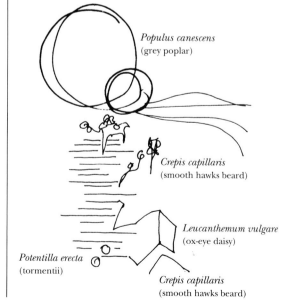

Populus canescens
(grey poplar)

Crepis capillaris
(smooth hawks beard)

Leucanthemum vulgare
(ox-eye daisy)

Potentilla erecta
(tormentii)

Crepis capillaris
(smooth hawks beard)

Left: An elevation which locates the plants in the grouping on the opposite page – a beautiful natural association that has both textural qualities and harmonious colour in flower and foliage.

THE LINK WITH YOUR SURROUND

My premise is that if we are of a region we do not want to be visually divided from it. A view, however meagre, of its landscape is part of a basic concept and this transition from pastoral into garden is often to do with planting.

Shaping the ground can help. The ha-ha ditch, a rather grand eighteenth-century technique, can work on a much reduced and cheaper scale, but it probably should not be accompanied by a planting of exotics.

It is perfectly valid for a garden with a rural view to be in phases with natives on its outer perimeters, their hybrid forms as you move towards the house and a gradual change to plants other than natives in association with the house itself. The plants that grow naturally on the parameter are managed; more intense hor-

ticultural techniques are only used on those that are near the house.

This is very different to the current fashion for 'pushing out' with intensive techniques: striping the lawn to the parameter, when it could be rough with wild flowers; and surrounding it with a golden conifer hedge when the hedgerow look – perhaps thickened with holly or yew – would be far more in keeping with what exists already.

Parameters were not always planted to keep the world and its prying eyes at bay. They were often grown as wind-breaks and the prevailing wind should be thoroughly researched before you do anything drastic by way of felling. A thinning rather than a felling will often break and filter the wind.

An alternative is to open up at a distance, then

Plan of the planting on the opposite page. It shows a considered, man-made plant grouping in the cottage garden idiom – but a cottage garden by the sea. Plants have to withstand both wind and a strongly saline atmosphere.

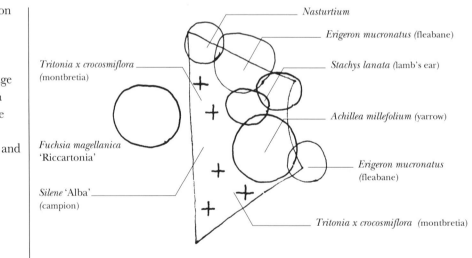

Tritonia x crocosmiflora (montbretia)

Fuchsia magellanica 'Riccartonia'

Silene 'Alba' (campion)

Nasturtium

Erigeron mucronatus (fleabane)

Stachys lanata (lamb's ear)

Achillea millefolium (yarrow)

Erigeron mucronatus (fleabane)

Tritonia x crocosmiflora (montbretia)

Salt-laden seaside air and wind are a difficult combination with which to compete horticulturally. This low decorative group seems to borrow its style from a natural association; plant groups drift one into another and there is nothing too harsh or strident. Rocks and pebbles were collected from the sea-shore to make walls and a traditional form of paving.

plant to filter the wind in the foreground where you see through and under trees. Birch, or a similar tree of light growth, works well this way.

So much for theoretical considerations. Now try to apply these to your site.

One of the easiest ways is to take photographs of your layout, enlarge them if necessary and, using tracing-paper, draw masses to indicate the planting you envisage in five or ten years time. Use simple circles for trees and smaller amalgams of circles for shrubs – botanical drafting skills are not called for. You will begin to get a feel for scale, for the mass and void and hence for proportion.

Start to think on paper. Then translate your thoughts into reality by putting stakes in the ground for individual trees. You will be establishing the bones of your layout, relating the scale of what you want to do inside your site to what is outside it.

PRACTICAL CONSIDERATIONS

As you start to build up your planting plan your choice of material to fulfil your ultimate objective will be tempered by practicality.

Most people are aware of the general characteristics of their surroundings. They will say that they live on the Chilterns (chalky), in Kent (clay) on the edge of a moor (acid), in a valley (wet), next to woods (shady), near the sea (windy), that they can or cannot grow rhododendrons which need an acid soil, and so on.

In fact each area will be a combination of more than one factor. To determine and/or assess your site is known as making a site analysis. Obviously your soil is a major guide.

A knowledge of its type is essential, for it is the common denominator between your garden and its location. Very simple kits for testing the acidity or alkalinity of soil are available from garden centres. They measure the hydrogen ion concentration of a suspension of soil in distilled water and give a reading which is expressed as a pH value. A pH value of 7 indicates an even or neutral balance; an ideal garden soil has one of 6.5. Figures higher than pH 7 indicate the degree of alkalinity or chalk. A reading below neutral indicates its acidity. Larger gardens, or smaller ones on a slope, may have different pH readings in different places.

After testing your soil for its pH value your assessment should include considering its general condition. In all probability this will have been adjusted by man from its original state. Waterlogging of a new site is common when the soil has been compacted, or a soil may be starved through neglect with no natural build-up of organic matter. An increasing problem is the level of the water table. The natural line of groundwater beneath the surface layer of the soil is being reduced so that what was a damp or moist soil becomes dry, altering its basic form and the vegetation and life dependent upon it.

Other elements of your site analysis will, of course, include its existing vegetation, its orientation to the sun, its prevailing wind and whether it is on very wet or exposed ground.

Armed with this knowledge, you can start to eliminate what would not be appropriate, selecting plant material to fulfil certain functions in chronological order.

In garden terms the order of selection is from large to small. In natural growing terms, looked at ecologically, it works from small to large. The gardener seeks an instant profile while nature builds hers up over time from herb through shrub to small, and then forest, tree.

The time factor must be taken into consideration. The town gardener can demand (and pay for) an instant effect to create a 'look' tomorrow. The fact that he or she will have to start thinning on the day after tomorrow is not a problem.

The suburban gardener will work on a five- or ten-year time span and probably needs much more material than the town gardener to achieve an effect. He or she will therefore buy smaller plants which reach maturity comparatively

These three diagrams illustrate the build-up of a plant group for acid soil. Space your plants according to how quickly you wish to create a solid look.

Thinking a grouping logically through like this helps to cut down on the inappropriate impulse buy.

Trees and evergreens provide the bones or skeleton of a layout.

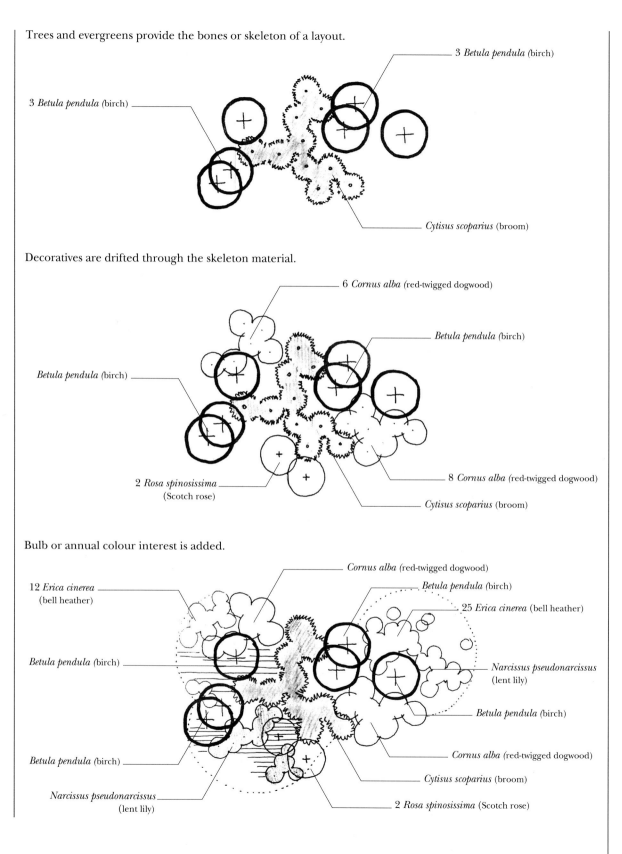

3 *Betula pendula* (birch)

3 *Betula pendula* (birch)

Cytisus scoparius (broom)

Decoratives are drifted through the skeleton material.

6 *Cornus alba* (red-twigged dogwood)

Betula pendula (birch)

Betula pendula (birch)

2 *Rosa spinosissima*
(Scotch rose)

8 *Cornus alba* (red-twigged dogwood)

Cytisus scoparius (broom)

Bulb or annual colour interest is added.

Cornus alba (red-twigged dogwood)

12 *Erica cinerea*
(bell heather)

Betula pendula (birch)

25 *Erica cinerea* (bell heather)

Betula pendula (birch)

Narcissus pseudonarcissus
(lent lily)

Betula pendula (birch)

Betula pendula (birch)

Cornus alba (red-twigged dogwood)

Narcissus pseudonarcissus
(lent lily)

Cytisus scoparius (broom)

2 *Rosa spinosissima* (Scotch rose)

quickly. The time span dictates the distances between plants and hence the number of individuals in groupings.

The country gardener's time span may be longer still. It depends on what is planted, where it is sited, and what it is associated with. Large existing trees and wide views need an eye for large-scale design. If you are planting forest trees they should be considered in terms of five, ten, twenty, fifty and even a hundred years. You can plant other material between them and fell it at certain intervals. But if you are placing special trees like walnuts you will see them in your mind's eye as stately, single specimens. Beech and oak are either grouped or single in the countryside. Judge planting distances carefully. In parkland, for instance, they will be different to distances in a woodland screen or shelter belt.

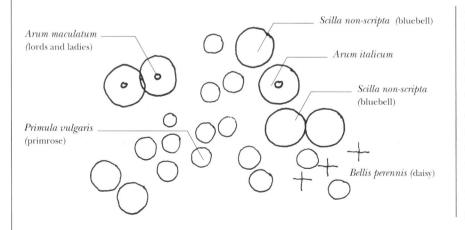

Arum maculatum (lords and ladies)

Scilla non-scripta (bluebell)

Arum italicum

Scilla non-scripta (bluebell)

Primula vulgaris (primrose)

Bellis perennis (daisy)

Above: This grouping illustrates a looser placement of primroses (*Primula vulgaris*) and daisies (*Bellis perennis*), with bluebells (*Scilla non-scripta*) and leaves of lords and ladies (*Arum maculatum*). One type is drifted through another.

Left: Plan of the grouping above.

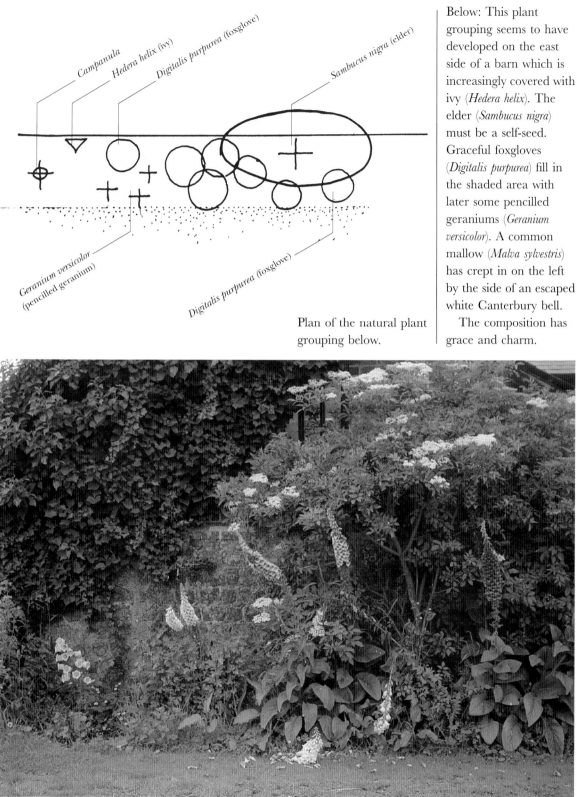

Campanula Hedera helix (ivy) Digitalis purpurea (foxglove) Sambucus nigra (elder)

Geranium versicolor
(pencilled geranium)

Digitalis purpurea (foxglove)

Plan of the natural plant grouping below.

Below: This plant grouping seems to have developed on the east side of a barn which is increasingly covered with ivy (*Hedera helix*). The elder (*Sambucus nigra*) must be a self-seed. Graceful foxgloves (*Digitalis purpurea*) fill in the shaded area with later some pencilled geraniums (*Geranium versicolor*). A common mallow (*Malva sylvestris*) has crept in on the left by the side of an escaped white Canterbury bell.

The composition has grace and charm.

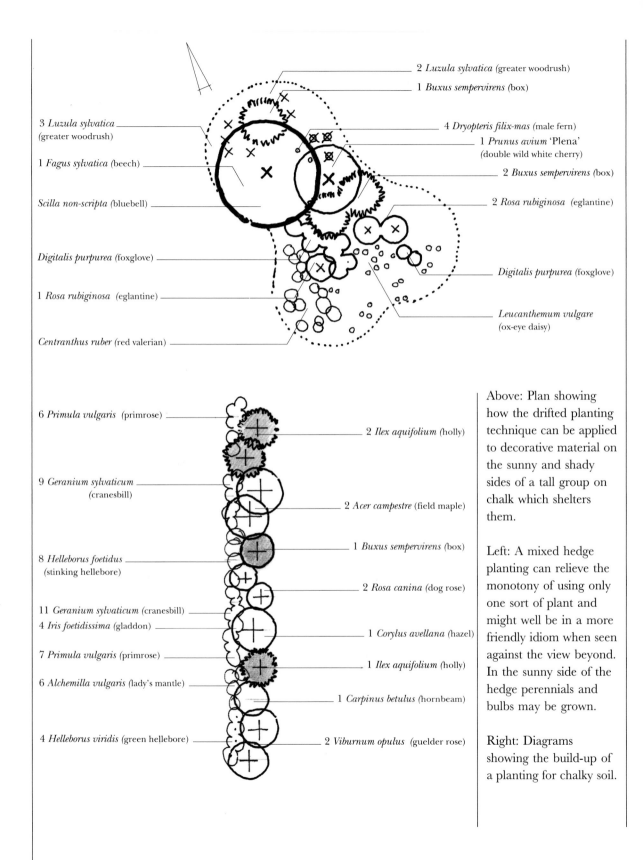

3 *Luzula sylvatica* (greater woodrush)

1 *Fagus sylvatica* (beech)

Scilla non-scripta (bluebell)

Digitalis purpurea (foxglove)

1 *Rosa rubiginosa* (eglantine)

Centranthus ruber (red valerian)

2 *Luzula sylvatica* (greater woodrush)

1 *Buxus sempervirens* (box)

4 *Dryopteris filix-mas* (male fern)

1 *Prunus avium* 'Plena' (double wild white cherry)

2 *Buxus sempervirens* (box)

2 *Rosa rubiginosa* (eglantine)

Digitalis purpurea (foxglove)

Leucanthemum vulgare (ox-eye daisy)

6 *Primula vulgaris* (primrose)

9 *Geranium sylvaticum* (cranesbill)

8 *Helleborus foetidus* (stinking hellebore)

11 *Geranium sylvaticum* (cranesbill)
4 *Iris foetidissima* (gladdon)

7 *Primula vulgaris* (primrose)

6 *Alchemilla vulgaris* (lady's mantle)

4 *Helleborus viridis* (green hellebore)

2 *Ilex aquifolium* (holly)

2 *Acer campestre* (field maple)

1 *Buxus sempervirens* (box)

2 *Rosa canina* (dog rose)

1 *Corylus avellana* (hazel)

1 *Ilex aquifolium* (holly)

1 *Carpinus betulus* (hornbeam)

2 *Viburnum opulus* (guelder rose)

Above: Plan showing how the drifted planting technique can be applied to decorative material on the sunny and shady sides of a tall group on chalk which shelters them.

Left: A mixed hedge planting can relieve the monotony of using only one sort of plant and might well be in a more friendly idiom when seen against the view beyond. In the sunny side of the hedge perennials and bulbs may be grown.

Right: Diagrams showing the build-up of a planting for chalky soil.

Trees and shrubs form the skeleton of the planting.

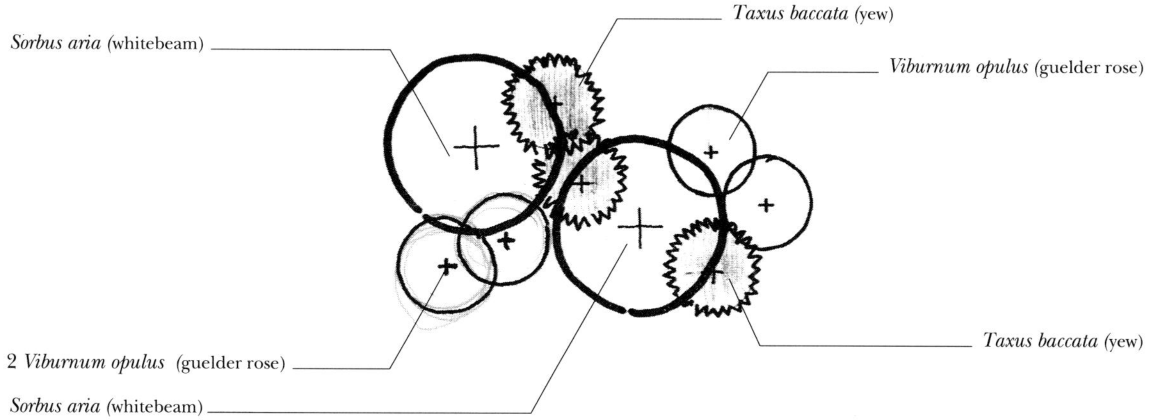

Taxus baccata (yew)

Sorbus aria (whitebeam)

Viburnum opulus (guelder rose)

2 Viburnum opulus (guelder rose)

Taxus baccata (yew)

Sorbus aria (whitebeam)

Decoratives are drifted through the skeletal planting.

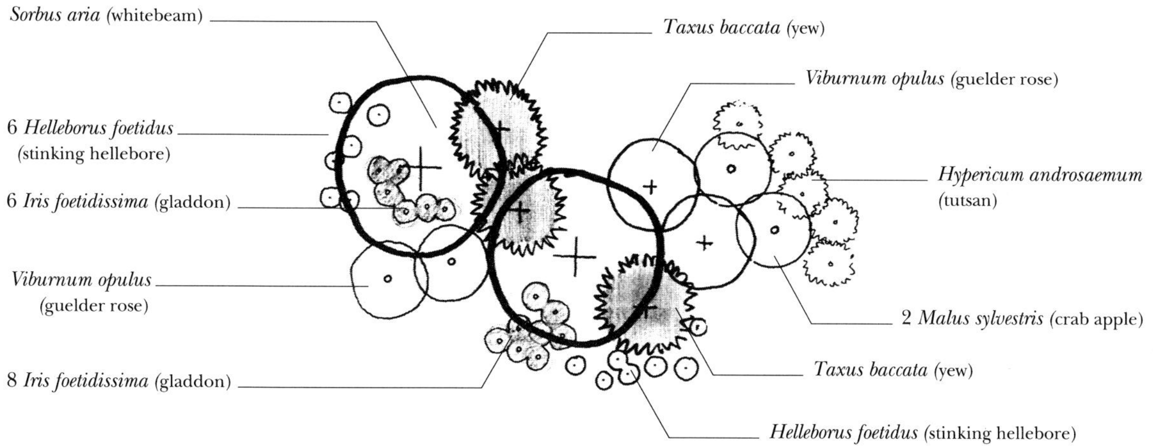

Sorbus aria (whitebeam)

Taxus baccata (yew)

Viburnum opulus (guelder rose)

6 Helleborus foetidus
(stinking hellebore)

6 Iris foetidissima (gladdon)

Hypericum androsaemum
(tutsan)

Viburnum opulus
(guelder rose)

8 Iris foetidissima (gladdon)

2 Malus sylvestris (crab apple)

Taxus baccata (yew)

Helleborus foetidus (stinking hellebore)

Colour interest is added.

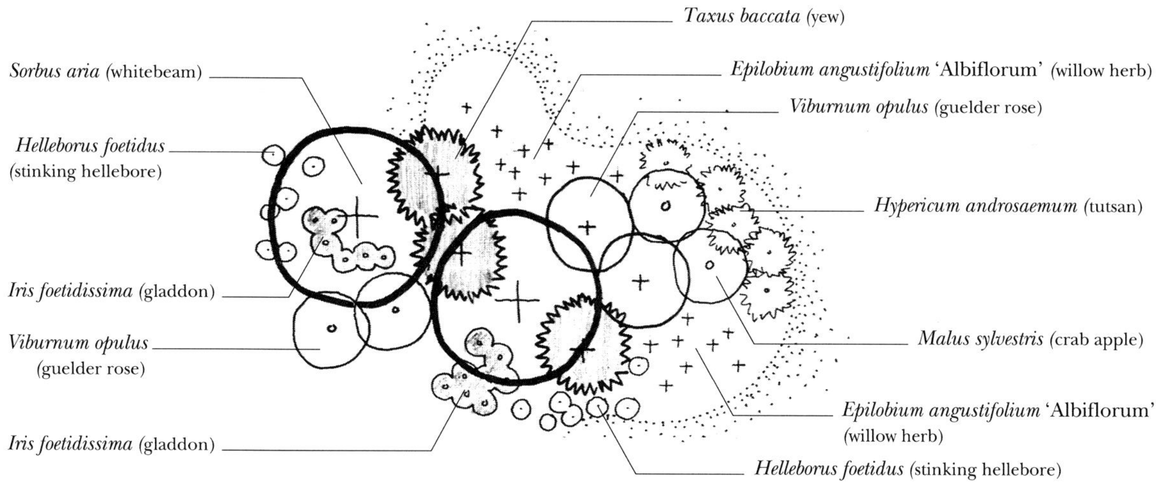

Taxus baccata (yew)

Epilobium angustifolium 'Albiflorum' (willow herb)

Sorbus aria (whitebeam)

Viburnum opulus (guelder rose)

Helleborus foetidus
(stinking hellebore)

Hypericum androsaemum (tutsan)

Iris foetidissima (gladdon)

Viburnum opulus
(guelder rose)

Malus sylvestris (crab apple)

Epilobium angustifolium 'Albiflorum'
(willow herb)

Iris foetidissima (gladdon)

Helleborus foetidus (stinking hellebore)

TREES: THE STARTING-POINT

Start with trees that might be classed as the specials: the one-offs. If you already have a tree or trees, think carefully before adding more.

The specials in a suburban garden may not necessarily be forest trees. If large specimens outside your site are visual elements in your landscape you can scale down their size through medium-sized trees.

Depending on soil, orientation and local suitability you might select wild cherry (*Prunus avium*) or bird cherry (*P. padus*). Both flower and subsequently fruit and are often seen at the edge of native woodland. Whitebeam (*Sorbus aria*) and mountain ash (*S. aucuparia*) are tough and decorative and become medium-sized trees. Whitebeam looks wonderful on the edges of downland with dark yew or box. Mountain ash stands wind and exposure in moorland locations.

The alders (*Alnus* sp.) are handsome trees with spring catkins. They prefer a damp situation.

Both the black and grey poplar (*Populus nigra* and *P. canescens*) occur throughout the country. They are excellent in a screen planting. The black poplar is fairly coarse in growth, while the grey poplar suckers like mad. This can be an advantage when space is available, and the growth can be contrasted with evergreen.

Our common silver birch (*Betula pendula*) and endless other forms of the species are among our most popular trees. Planting a successful grouping is not necessarily easy: birches naturally occur fairly close together and the standard forms include double- and triple-stemmed specimens. However, a good planting is spectacular throughout the year.

The association of lush southern birch on home counties common land is very different to that of the armies of birch that reach up glens and corries into quite open moorland where the top specimens become stunted with wind.

Left: The winter beauty of tree and shrub shapes is enhanced with a gentle frosting.

Right: Our native trees, well-selected, can provide just as much interest as many exotic species – and further, they sit better in the landscape. Against a background of beech, whitebeam (*Sorbus aria*) shows up well against yew (*Taxus baccata*). There is blackthorn or sloe (*Prunus spinosa*) scrub in front.

SKELETAL PLANTING

Start to build up a skeleton of shrubs and small trees. This grouping need not necessarily be decorative. Rather, it must be functional: screening, sheltering, holding, partitioning. A plant needs to be evergreen to perform this function at all times, and we have few natives. Exotics can therefore be mixed with strong-growing deciduous shrubs. The natives will grow faster than the exotics and can be thinned later.

It is difficult to draw the dividing line between native and exotic. I am inclined to consider as native anything that does not look exotic. And introduced plants that have been grown here for centuries must be nearly native, if not truly so. Laurustinus (*Viburnum tinus*), a native of southeastern Europe, is a case in point. It is a vital evergreen for skeletal planting and with it I would include the cherry laurel (*Laurocerasus officinalis*), originally from eastern Europe and Asia Minor, which grows well in shade.

Our native evergreen trees are Scots pine (*Pinus sylvestris*), the evergreen or holm oak (*Quercus ilex*) and yew (*Taxus baccata*). On chalk there is the common juniper (*Juniper communis*) and our native holly (*Ilex aquifolium*). Coming down in scale we have native box (*Buxus sempervirens*), common privet (*Ligustrum vulgare*) and, in favoured places, the strawberry tree (*Arbutus unedo*) – very much a special.

Of the fast-growing deciduous shrubs, I would include guelder rose (*Viburnum opulus*), the wayfaring tree (*Viburnum lantana*) and the common spindle tree (*Euonymus europaeus*) with hazel (*Corylus avellana*), dogwoods (*Cornus sanguinea* or *C. alba*) and eglantine (*Rosa rubiginosa*). Near the sea use buckthorn (*Rhamnus catharticus*) or sea buckthorn (*Hippophae rhamnoides*).

The host of small deciduous trees that will thicken up your skeletal planting include the

native crab apple (*Malus sylvestris*), pear (*Pyrus communis*), wild cherry (*Prunus avium*) and bullace plum (*Prunus institia*). Many shrubby willows and thorns are tough for hard conditions.

The number of plants of each variety depends on scale. Broadly, use fewer groups of more in

number. This is not decorative planting; it is gardening in imitation of nature. She generally drifts her material – or uses great swathes of one particular plant. Only in a meadow does she create a scattered effect of annuals and biennials through grasses.

Although the planting of this garden is not in the country idiom it does show the value of evergreen materials in winter, which provide bones and a dark background.

THE DECORATIVE SHRUB LAYER

When you are seeking to create a more natural effect using native plant material, the decorative layer should not be seen as the foreground to a shrub border as in an exotic garden. Instead, groupings of shrubs that are decorative at certain times of the year should punctuate and enhance their backdrop of existing or new skeletal material. The decoratives associate well with our small range of native evergreens, and this association looks good in smaller gardens.

The decorative shrub layer will probably be smaller in growth than the rampant bulky shrubs and their charm will not necessarily be in their flowers, as in the exotic garden. Rather, it lies in the colour and form of their foliage, their autumn and stem colour and their berries. Even their dead fruit or flower forms have a ghostly charm as winter approaches. Any one plant may combine these virtues, but they will be less obvious in native specimens than in those which have been hybridized and deciduous shrubs are best accompanied by wild flowers and bulbs.

We have a good range of native roses, and it is legitimate to use them in association with hybrid forms that have not become too bright.

The dog rose (*Rosa canina*), the common form of one of our most beautiful hedgerow plants, has abundant rose hips in late summer. Sweet briar or eglantine (*R. rubiginosa*) differs from it by having a denser growth and leaflets that are sweetly scented when rubbed. Its flowers are fragrant and its rose hips are bigger and more rounded. The Scotch or Burnet rose (*R. spinosissima*) does not grow very high, spreads well and grows on sandy heaths, even near the sea. Its flowers are pink or white. Several varieties have insignificant rose hips. The foliage of most shrubby roses turns red-gold in autumn.

I am very fond of the broom family whose

A period house clothed with decorative climbers is set among swathes of shrub roses with an edging of cow parsley. While only the roses and cow parsley are native, the generosity of the *Wisteria sinensis* blends well with them. The rose against the house is a form of dog rose (*Rosa canina*). Among the shrub roses is the fragrant-leafed sweet briar or eglantine (*Rosa rubiginosa*).

native form (*Cytisus scoparius*) is bright yellow. A robust, fast-growing shrub, broom has good foliage form, particularly if it is clipped after flowering so that it does not become too leggy. It is one of the few native shrubs that gives architectural form to a grouping. Butcher's broom (*Ruscus aculeatus*) has an odd form but grows in the driest shade.

There are one or two forms of deciduous hypericum and many species within the genus. One of the most handsome native forms is commonly called tutsan (a corruption of '*tente-saine*'

or 'heal all'). It is a very useful shade plant with yellow flowers – like all hypericums – and good seed-heads through winter.

The dogwoods (*Cornus sanguinea* and *C. alba*) are good, robust, infill plants. If they are kept stooled down, or are cut to ground level each spring, their one-year wood has lovely winter colour and good twiggy form. Another decorative, autumn-berrying shrub, whose hybrids I would have no hesitation in using, is snowberry (*Symphoricarpos*).

For acid soils, there are ericas and heathers, bog myrtle (*Myrica gale*) and the ground-covering bilberry (*Vaccinium myrtillus*).

A personal favourite is spurge laurel (*Daphne laureola*). It prefers a slightly alkaline soil and is an erect, evergreen shrub no more than 1m (3ft) high. The unfragrant green flowers it bears in spring blend well with crisp green foliage. However, it seems to be fairly short-lived.

The native barberry (*Berberis vulgare*) grows up to several feet in hedges or copses. It fell into disfavour when it was discovered that it could play host to the spoors of rust – a disease of wheat.

WILD FLOWERS

By far the largest group of native plants is our wild flowers, many of which are the parents of our most popular perennials. Indeed, they were cultivated from earliest times in cottage gardens, often for their medicinal properties. They have been bred up over the generations and the cultivated forms often lack the simple charm of their early ancestors.

For the uninitiated, flowers come in various forms according to their growth pattern. An annual grows from seed to flowering and then dies within one season and a biennial takes two years to complete the same process. A perennial goes on and on, from year to year, sending out side shoots and growing away from its original centre. In traditional flower gardens, perennials that have grown out from their original position are divided each autumn – a time-consuming process.

When you add wild flower masses – 'the pretties' – to tree and shrub plantings to make up a composition, start by drifting them through the decorative layer. If they like where you have placed them they will probably self-seed. Remember, you are looking at how plant masses occur naturally in meadow, scrub or woodland, not in neat Edwardian borders. If a plant likes its situation it will propagate itself and you will get drift and mass rather than tight little bundles of three, or five or seven specimens.

One of the pleasures of this layer is that the flowers seed themselves in all manner of unexpected places. These natural incidents give wilder gardens a spontaneity that many more self-conscious ones lack. Lady's mantle (*Alchemilla vulgaris*), mullein (*Verbascum thrapsus*) and foxgloves (*Digitalis purpurea*) are wild forms of more common garden varieties and self-seed liberally to create the spontaneous look.

The range of perennials from the wild is huge and must include the ox-eye daisy (*Leucanthemum vulgare*), a large range of cranesbills and wild geraniums including *Geranium phaeum*, *G. sanguineum* and *G. pratense*, aquilegia, the stinking hellebore (*Helleborus foetidus*), bugle (*Ajuga reptans*), purple loosestrife (*Lythrum salicaria*), yarrows

This is the flowering of a native annual cornfield, now available as a seed mixture for sowing although the plants were once common in arable fields. Such a mix can be used for companion sowing with a meadow mix of perennials that will flank it at a later time the following year. Flowers in the native cornfield mix include cornflowers, corn chamomile, corn marigold and corn cockle.

(*Achillea millefolium*), and euphorbias in plenty. There are also scabious (*Succisa pratensis*), various primulas and violets, red valerian (*Centranthus ruber*), feverfew (*Tanacetum parthenium*) and, for larger areas, rosebay willow herb (*Epilobium angustifolium*).

I enjoy Scotch thistle (*Onopordum acanthium*) and

milk thistle (*Silybum marianum*), but both of these are biennial.

Wild flowers, like other plants, have optimum requirements for soil and drainage, light or shade, and do not grow naturally over the whole country. Some of their major requirements are in the list at the end of the book.

NATIVE BULBS

Although we do not have a large number of true native bulbs, introduced species have become naturalized over the generations.

There are two very beautiful native anemones: the pasque-flower (*Anemone pulsatilla*) of chalky pastures and the wood anemone (*A. nemerosa*). Other natives include snowdrops (*Galanthus nivalis*) and their big sister the later spring snowflake (*Leucojum vernum*), the English bluebell (*Scilla non-scripta*) and the harebell (*Campanula rotundifolia*) known as the Scotch bluebell. Our native narcissi − the lent lily (*N. pseudonarcissus*) and the Tenby daffodil (*N. obvallaris*) − have a fine simplicity and can withstand spring winds. The snake's head fritillary (*Fritillaria meleagris*), which flowers in spring in chalky meadowland, is a beauty. Also in spring there are sheets of ramsons or wild garlic (*Allium ursinum*) in woodland shade, often with bluebells. In limestone woodland you will find the lovely Solomon's seal (*Polygonatum multiflorum*). There is also the woodland-growing lily of the valley (*Convallaria majalis*) with delicious scented flowers.

The winter aconite (*Eranthis hyemalis*) is not a true native, but it is an established wild spring bulb and naturalizes itself in great sheets of early yellow. At the other end of the year, autumn colchicums and crocus are now naturalized.

Lastly, there are yellow flag irises, the winter-berrying *Iris foetidissima* and cuckoo pint or lords and ladies (*Arum maculatum*).

This gentle grouping is a lesson in how to space and drift bulbs in general. It shows the snowdrop (*Galanthus nivalis*) with winter aconite (*Eranthis hyemalis*), the yellow flower on the left, and the little *Cyclamen hederifolium*. In the foreground is the self-seeding *Crocus tomasinianus*.

THE WILD HEDGE

The mixed hedge is a more formal way to create a background – and one that takes up less space. Use holly (*Ilex*) with hazel (*Corylus*), hawthorn (*Crataegus*), the dog rose (*Rosa canina*) and the viburnums on chalk. Blackthorn (*Prunus spinosa*) and field maple (*Acer campestre*) may also be used. Depending on orientation, plant ferns or primula in the shade of a wild hedge. Any number of wild flowers will succeed on the sunny side.

By far the greatest part of our hedgerows is made up of hawthorn, which was planted because of its prickles. There are two types. The most common is *Crataegus monogyna* but there is also Midland hawthorn, (*C. oxyacantha*), which has larger leaves. Hawthorn flowers generously in May, loading its branches with pink or white blossom that looks like snow. In autumn it furnishes hedgerows with the same generosity of haw fruits which provide valuable food for birds into the new year.

Blackthorn or sloe (*Prunus spinosa*) is also heavily armed with thorns and has fine white early flowers and very characteristic tart fruit.

At one time it was the practice to allow standard trees – mainly oak or ash – to develop at regular intervals along a hedgerow to give shelter to cattle in the field that the hedge enclosed. But arable land does not need shade and this practice was abandoned even before that of ripping out the hedge to allow for greater manouvrability of agricultural machinery was introduced.

A decorative 'wild' hedge at an entrance can be attractive. This one is composed of elder (*Sambucus nigra*), dog rose (*Rosa canina*) and sweet briar (*Rosa rubiginosa*). At its base is cow parsley (*Anthriscus sylvestris*) and blue-flowering comfrey (*Symphytum officinale*), which I find invasive.

GRASSES

A whole range of material is becoming increasingly popular and typifies the type of plant that can combine country with garden. It is the decorative grasses, which link in with out visually with a softness and grace that can give shrub groupings an added textural quality.

Grasses are not easy to use. Planting a single clump on its own or among shrubs can be unsettling, for grasses naturally grow *en masse*, giving the effect of waste, scrubland or the waving softness of a cornfield or prairie.

Although our native grasses are not nearly as spectacular as imported ones they can nevertheless add the softness and texture that a group of native shrubs alone might lack. Furthermore, there are native grasses, rushes or sedges for most situations. Some are fairly rampant so care must be taken when selecting them.

Quaking grass (*Briza media*) is the most beautiful of our wild grasses with delicate seed-heads from June to August. Cyperus sedge (*Carex pseudocyperus*) is for all damp boggy areas. Tufted hair grass (*Deschampsia caespitosa*) is about 1 m (3 ft) high with soft, fluffy seed-heads. Tall fescue (*Festuca arundinacea*) is architectural and good for acid soil. Yorkshire fog (*Holcus lanatus*) has pinky mauve flowers. Meadow barley (*Hordium murinum*) has typical weeping heads as it ripens.

The soft rush (*Juncus effusus*) is perfect for all damp areas, and equally good in semi-shade. The great woodrush (*Luzula sylvatica*) has a branched, spreading flower-head and Timothy or catstail (*Phleum pratense*) has stiff, tufted flower-spikes.

Grasses keep their seed-heads throughout winter, softening the winter stems of deciduous trees and shrubs.

CLIMBERS

Ivy (*Hedera helix*) is one of the commonest ground covers in woodland, and often invades trees. It is probably too rampant for most gardens, although its hybrid and variegated forms are very handsome and can look wonderful with snowdrops growing through them.

Honeysuckle or woodbine (*Lonicera periclymenum*) is probably our most lovely climbing shrub with delicious sweetly scented flowers. It looks good rambling over a fence or outhouse, but can strangle weaker host shrubs.

Traveller's joy or old man's beard (*Clematis vitalba*) is commonest on calcareous soils, where it drapes the hedgerows. It can be vigorous. Its small, greenish flowers are insignificant but its curly grey seed-heads are spectacular in winter.

In the romantic garden honeysuckle and roses romp through gnarled old trees, producing cascades of flowers from along their branches. Actually it is the climbers – particularly honeysuckle – that create the gnarl if they start to grow inside woody vegetation which is not yet tough enough to withstand their strangling growth. This shrubby honeysuckle or woodbine (*Lonicera periclymenum*) on an old stump will need support before it begins to ramble on its own. It is a rampant twiner, but worth it for the scent of its flowers.

FERNS

There is a good range of native ferns for cool shady places, beneath trees and under north walls. However, they do not like wind or drought so their soil must be enriched with compost leaf or leafmould.

One of the commonest ferns in damp woodlands is the hart's tongue fern (*Asplenium scolopendrium*) with its leathery, strap-like foliage. In contrast, the lady fern (*Athyrium filix-femina*) has finely divided fronds which may grow to over a metre (3 ft) in moist, shaded conditions. A good deciduous all-rounder is the buckler fern (*Dryopteris affinis*). Many varieties are in cultivation, one of which, the male fern (*Dryopteris filix-mas*), has tall, upright feathery fronds and is excellent for woodland or wild plantings.

The oak fern (*Gymnocarpium dryopteris*) is excellent for stony woodland where it forms a dense mat. The royal fern (*Osmunda regalis*) grows to between 1 m and 2 m (3 ft and 6 ft) and is our largest native fern. It needs moisture and coolness all summer. There are a number of varieties of the common polypody fern (*Polypodium vulgare*). Very adaptable, it grows in almost any conditions but prefers stony ground.

Ferns mix well with Solomon's seal, lily of the valley and primulas in cool shade.

There is something very cooling about the thought of ferns in the dappled shade of woodland on a summer's day, and, given the right conditions, they are easy to grow. Surrounding this woodland pool in Vann Gardens, Surrey, are fountains of male fern (*Dryopteris filix-mas*) with, on the left, the emergent fronds of the royal fern (*Osmunda regalis*).

PUTTING PLANTS IN THEIR PLACES

The gardens on the following pages have been chosen because they are in harmony with the landscape in which they stand. In making my selection I concentrated first on the planting – the theme of this book. But the trees, shrubs and flowers always overlay a design and this too is expressive of its site, reflecting what the owners wanted to see in their garden, the amount they wanted to spend and the time they were prepared to give to maintaining the garden.

In their haste owners of new gardens often seek a layout and/or a planting solution for their site too soon. Savour your site before going to the expense of altering it. You will discover where the winds or draughts come from, the height of the sun in summer and winter, who and where the visually offending neighbours are, and exactly what your soil will grow.

Take time to study the trees, shrubs and flowers that grow naturally in your area so that when you start to plan your garden you will know which plants to put in their right places.

A good example of a garden
layout blending into the
countryside.

A GARDEN NEAR THE COAST

Left: The cottage stands in splendid isolation, with the Atlantic not more than a quarter-mile away. Wind rushes up the valley. In the lee of the house and knoll some form of natural garden is to be attempted, terminating in the foreground hillside cleft.

Right: These diagrams show the design process, from initial sketch to detailed planting in elevation.

The approach to this house in the West Country is spectacular. Suddenly it is there, nestling in a fold of the land with the Atlantic beyond, and as you proceed downhill from the windswept hilltop the vegetation becomes more and more lush. It starts with bracken the height of a man and spires of purple foxgloves. Standing scraggy thorn and sloe appear, then willow scrub and, last, some stunted oaks before the windy knoll on which the slate-and-cob house sits.

This is an artist's home, appreciated for its isolation, its proximity to the sea and, in the spring, the myriad clifftop flowers that flourish in the alkaline soil and brilliant light and survive even the salt-laden gale force winds, hugging the crevices and flattening themselves into the soft sward. For herbs and wild flowers are the glory of this coast and are seen at their best through April, May and June.

But wild flowers do not a shelter make, and the owners of the old fisherman-cum-farmer's house wanted a still corner in which to escape the constant wind that is channelled up their valley from the sea. A still corner in which to sit and − even more − to plant. For they have the gardener's twitch to meddle, adjust, even 'improve' upon what nature intended.

The planning and planting of such a project could easily be a disaster. Few exotics will grow in such specific conditions and if alien materials were imported for the terrace and wall they would stick out like a sore thumb.

This was to be a test case for the vernacular garden and the design process started with an exploration of the area, seeing and feeling the house in its setting and determining not to impose upon that.

The next stage was to photograph the site and, using tracing-paper over a enlarged print, start to sketch in the terrace and planting profiles. The rolling, organic landscape calls for curves and even the grouping of the buildings cleaves into the

I traced the outline of the house and knoll from photographs. Steps lead down to the garden but I suggested running a terrace round the base of the knoll above the meadow and will plant above it.

This shows the vegetation as I would ultimately like to see it. There is a small open 'field' for spring bulbs and wild flowers.

The sketch above has been interpreted into a planting elevation.

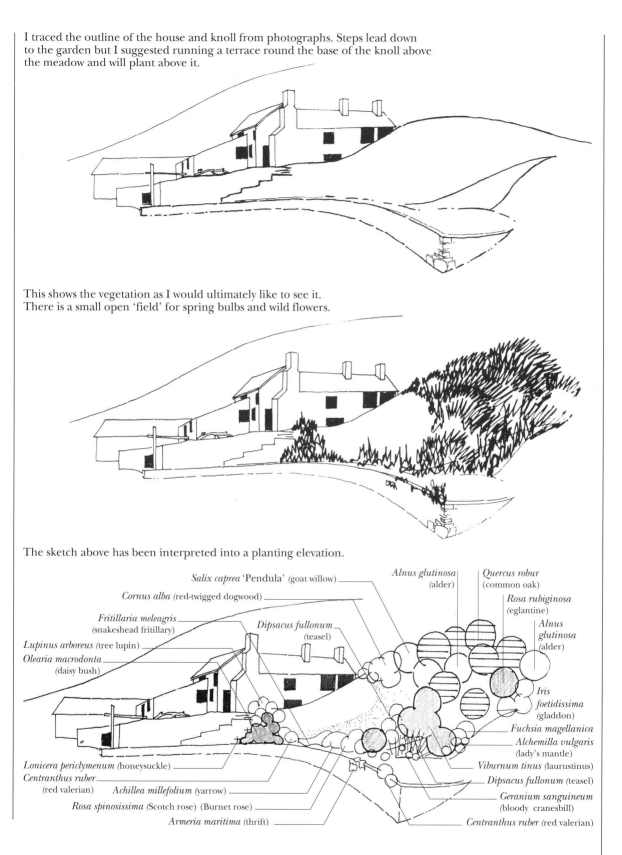

Salix caprea 'Pendula' (goat willow)

Cornus alba (red-twigged dogwood)

Alnus glutinosa (alder)

Quercus robur (common oak)

Rosa rubiginosa (eglantine)

Fritillaria meleagris (snakeshead fritillary)

Dipsacus fullonum (teasel)

Alnus glutinosa (alder)

Lupinus arboreus (tree lupin)

Olearia macrodonta (daisy bush)

Iris foetidissima (gladdon)

Fuchsia magellanica

Alchemilla vulgaris (lady's mantle)

Lonicera periclymenum (honeysuckle)

Viburnum tinus (laurustinus)

Centranthus ruber (red valerian)

Dipsacus fullonum (teasel)

Achillea millefolium (yarrow)

Geranium sanguineum (bloody cranesbill)

Rosa spinosissima (Scotch rose) (Burnet rose)

Armeria maritima (thrift)

Centranthus ruber (red valerian)

hillside. Anything angular is naturally moulded by the strong winds.

So a terrace curves out from the house, in its lee for shelter, and above it on a gentle knoll a mixed planting of trees and shrubs with perennials, wild flowers and bulbs is planned. The pathway leads to a ferny outside room that is ideal for a sheltered read in summer sun.

There is a low wood a little way up the valley with moss-covered branches of oak, hazel and willow and the skeleton of the planting is similar to that of this native woodland: scrub oak (*Quercus robur*), alder (*Alnus glutinosa*) with goat willow (*Salix caprea*). Laurustinus (*Viburnum tinus*) was added for winter depth. Then came red-twigged dogwood (*Cornus alba*) for its stemmed effect, with sweet briar (*Rosa rubiginosa*) and Burnet rose (*Rosa spinosissima*). Against the house is a swathe of tree lupin (*Lupinus arboreus*) with, below it, the New Zealand daisy bush (*Olearia macrodonta*), a tough plant for seaside areas and understated enough to be acceptable. Climbing up the house wall is a fragrant honeysuckle, *Lonicera periclymenum*. Fuschia (*F. magellanica*) grows in the light shade of

Left: A spit of land divides the house from the sea which crashes into the soft shale and limestone cliffs. In springtime wild flowers grow in great drifts on the grassy hillside.

the ferny outside room at the end of the path. It makes hedges in mild parts of Ireland and the west of Wales.

Flower colour is introduced with foxgloves (*Digitalis purpurea*), wild geraniums (*Geranium sanguineum*) and valerian (*Centranthus ruber*), and thrift (*Armeria maritima*) in the walls with yarrow (*Achillea millefolium*.) Teazle (*Dipsacus fullonum*) is for winter. Bulbs include bluebells (*Scilla non-scripta*) and snake's head fritillary (*Fritillaria meleagris*) in the little lawn at the side of the house.

Other plants can be added later, but a framework has been established and with it the owners' horticultural urge can be assuaged.

Right: Steps in vernacular stonework lead down from the house. Note the use of driftwood and boulders from the shore. A similar terrace and retaining wall will run away to the right and the hillside above it will be planted.

A GARDEN IN A FARMYARD

I went to a summer party in this garden on a sunny evening and we sat in the old restored cart shed – its interior had been paved and gravelled – looking out and up to tumbling terraces of vegetation. To one side was a view of a neighbouring oast house. We were sitting in an old farmyard which Ryl Nowell, the designer and owner, had converted for her family.

Much of the plant material of which I was conscious was great thickets of grass: clumps of

Below: Overall plan of the garden that designer Ryl Nowell created at Wilderness Farm. Terraces run across it giving a stepped Italianate feel, though the planting is definitely English.

Right: A cart shed on the right has become an open loggia looking into a richly planted garden. Beyond it the roof of a traditional oast house completes the setting.

The tall plant is *Macleaya cordata*; it should only be used on a large scale, as it can become invasive.

By autumn the garden is really full. Grasses combine with fruits and shrubs to give a very special effect.

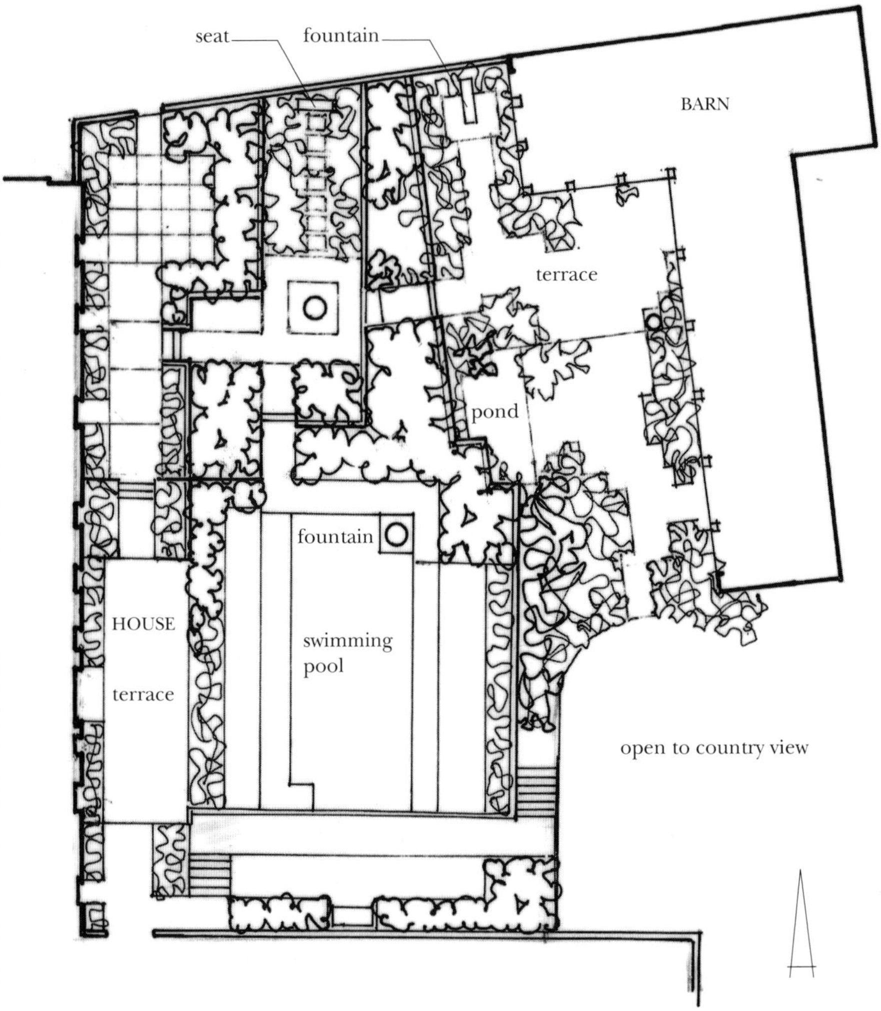

seat — fountain

BARN

terrace

pond

fountain

HOUSE

swimming pool

terrace

open to country view

Plants are in tight masses in spring, but there is an interesting interplay of foliage forms and textures – with little flower colour.

The large-leafed central plant is rheum, a member of the rhubarb family. A viburnum flowers in the centre of the garden with the huge purple leaves of *Ligularia clivorum* beneath it. There is also box, hosta and lady's mantle (*Alchemilla mollis*) with the striped leaves of *Iris pseudacorus* 'Variegata' – a handsome form of our native yellow flag, the water iris which grows in shallow water or marshy ground.

Stipa giganteum with *Carex flagelliflora*. They were laden with seed-heads which the sun was catching, and it was the first time that grasses, outside the United States of America, had caught my eye. I have since seen wonderful display beds of a range of grasses at both Kew and Wisley gardens. The grasses were, again, clumps of *S. giganteum*. Their disadvantage is that their fullness occurs only in late summer when they bear their seed-heads – but it does last through winter.

The remainder of the planting in the garden divides the space into 'rooms' at different levels with steps between them. One level contains a swimming pool. This is the sort of garden that can be truly described as 'tumbly' – and with lots of hidden corners.

Left: The transition from garden through to surrounding farmland is masterly, the cultivated garden blending into its rural background with complete ease.

Surrounding the barn on the left is *Buddleia globosa* with green-flowering *Euphorbia palustris*. In the foreground are the grey leaves of *Cynara cordunculus*.

A GARDEN WITH SCREEN PLANTING

A Victorian house commands this site and the original planting against the wall that runs away to the south is still there. It is evergreen oak (*Quercus ilex*) under which very little will grow.

The further end of the garden to the south had been sold and a house was being built there. Quick screening of the building operation with something that was green and decorative to look at from the house was an absolute priority; an enclosure for the swimming-pool was of secondary importance.

A small rose garden with a central feature leads the eye away from the building site, and the lower-growing trees and shrubs behind the roses will blend into the evergreen oaks.

The soil is very poor and alkaline and the basis of the screen is evergreen Portuguese laurel (*Prunus lusitanica*) with yew (*Taxus baccata*) planted at intervals of about 3 m (10 ft). Whitebeam (*Sorbus aria* 'Lutescens') with silver birch (*Betula pendula*), both of which have stem and foliage interest, grow through and over these hardy, shade-tolerant shrubs. Holly (*Ilex aquifolium*) with yellow-berried, fast-growing cotoneaster (*C. × rothschildianus*) completes the planting.

None of the plants will be high enough to shade the swimming pool but they will break the eyeline of the new building.

Left: The peeling grey bark of many forms of birch adds enormously to the textural quality of a garden. Here a silver birch (*Betula pendula*) has a backing of its own autumn-coloured leaves.

Above: Silver birch looks well when many stems grow together – as they do naturally. Here they are combined with early pussy willow heads (*Salix caprea*).

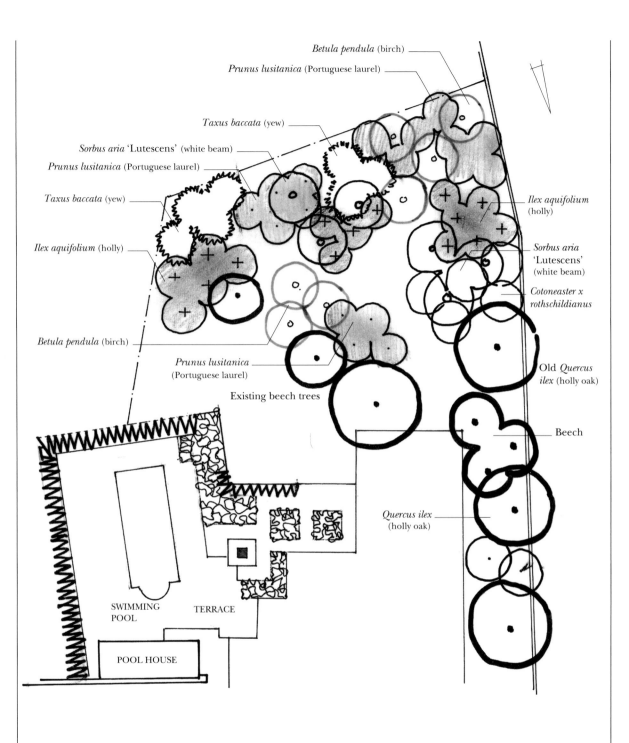

Betula pendula (birch)

Prunus lusitanica (Portuguese laurel)

Taxus baccata (yew)

Sorbus aria 'Lutescens' (white beam)

Prunus lusitanica (Portuguese laurel)

Taxus baccata (yew)

Ilex aquifolium (holly)

Betula pendula (birch)

Prunus lusitanica (Portuguese laurel)

Existing beech trees

Ilex aquifolium (holly)

Sorbus aria 'Lutescens' (white beam)

Cotoneaster x rothschildianus

Old Quercus ilex (holly oak)

Beech

Quercus ilex (holly oak)

SWIMMING POOL

TERRACE

POOL HOUSE

This overall plan shows how an evergreen screen gives privacy to the house at the north end of the site as well as to the swimming pool area on the left. The design adjacent to the pool surround has been strengthened with a formal garden and feature so that the eye is held from going straight up the site. The tree screen will eventually provide a good background to the pool area.

A GARDEN IN MEADOWLAND

At Eastgrove Cottage in the Midlands there is a perfect blending of a twentieth-century flower garden with a seventeenth-century yeoman farmer's cottage – within a working landscape. The three forms meet in a small space to create a charming evocation of the Romantic ideal. For not only is this a plantsman's garden (and a plantswoman's too), using a broad palette of available shrub and perennial material, it also has a random layout evocative of the past, with climbers through and over barns and outhouses. There is a spring meadow and there are vegetables and free-range fowl, all seen against a backdrop of fields studded with cattle, geese and

grazing ponies. The woodland beyond, originally native lime wood, is now hazel with oak.

The free-draining sandy loam is over sandstone and has probably been cultivated for generations. The Skinners have gardened here since 1970 and, although the area is a plant-lover's delight, there is no sense of it being a collector's showpiece. And although colour is used in a considered way, forming a chain of connected groupings blended through foliages, it is not self-conscious.

Herbaceous perennials form the bulk of the planting and include typical cottage species such as columbines and campanulas. There are paeonies with yarrow, sedums with asters, fleabane and

Right: The original seventeenth-century cottage has an extension but old and new blend well. The garden surrounding the house is divided into 'rooms' by a *Lonicera nitida* hedge, in front of which white valerian (*Centranthus ruber* 'Albus') is grouped with *Artemesia* 'Powis Castle'. An eryngium thistle is flowering on the left.

Right: A pathway leads from one garden area to another, beneath a rosy archway which, most importantly, frames a view of the meadow beyond. The view is not disturbed by massed herby foreground plantings of grey *Artemesia* 'Powis Castle', and purple sage (*Salvia purpurescens*) on the right. The flower on the left is a white form of our native valerian (*V. officinalis*).

Left: In the outer garden shrubs and an orchard of fruit trees blend with the surrounding meadow. The inner garden contains a lovely mix of cottage garden flowers.

Below: In the full flowering cottage garden there are good-sized masses of each subject so that they are in scale with the hedge backdrop, the apple tree and the view beyond.

feverfew, sea hollies and lady's mantle, ornamental sea kale and fluffy gypsophilia, heuchera and Shasta daisy mixed with mallow and annual mimulas. It is a cultivated meadow look – a cottage garden of today. Helping to create this glorious disarray are the biennials: honesty, foxglove, forget-me-not and mullein pop up where they will. In spring, double primroses, auriculas and laced polyanthus add cottage charm, preceded by snowdrops and hellebore masses with drifts of crocuses and daffodils.

This tapestry of plant material is held together by the semi-formal use of *Lonicera nitida* hedging which provides a clipped, green backdrop to the foreground interest.

Eastgrove Cottage garden melds together the rolling countryside in which it sits with the timber-framed house but is totally a creation of today.

A GARDEN IN FARMLAND

This nineteenth-century brick farmhouse on the borders of Gloucestershire and Worcestershire looks into an old plum orchard, one of hundreds that once grew in the area. It is a flattish landscape, with only a gentle roll and the soil is mostly alkaline clay. There is a strong prevailing south-west wind.

The new owners of this property replanted much of the plum orchard and wanted the alterations they made to the house and its immediate surroundings to be very much within the idiom of their area. Although their first priority was not gardening they did want something pleasant to look at.

The house is bordered on the east side by the orchard. To the south there is a quiet road and the relics of a field hedge. To the west, where the boundary is a small stream, there is a view of fields and farm buildings.

The best view, however, north of the site, is of a farm pond with a row of willows that had once been pollarded on the far side.

The rear lawn was altered by removing old, unsuitable trees and the field boundary to the orchard was brought nearer to the house. Levels were adjusted to allow a shallow grass bank filled with spring bulbs to run up to the orchard –

The overall plan of the farmhouse (right) shows the entrance and drive. The detailed plan (below) shows the planting that is seen as the garden is entered from the road.

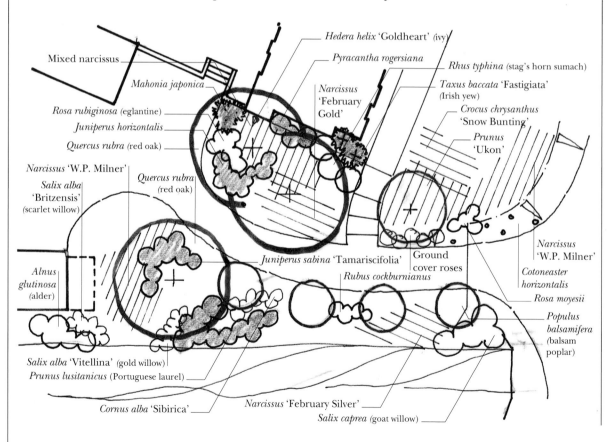

Mixed narcissus

Mahonia japonica

Rosa rubiginosa (eglantine)

Juniperus horizontalis

Quercus rubra (red oak)

Narcissus 'W.P. Milner'

Salix alba 'Britzensis' (scarlet willow)

Quercus rubra (red oak)

Alnus glutinosa (alder)

Salix alba 'Vitellina' (gold willow)

Prunus lusitanicus (Portuguese laurel)

Cornus alba 'Sibirica'

Hedera helix 'Goldheart' (ivy)

Pyracantha rogersiana

Rhus typhina (stag's horn sumach)

Narcissus 'February Gold'

Taxus baccata 'Fastigiata' (Irish yew)

Crocus chrysanthus 'Snow Bunting'

Prunus 'Ukon'

Juniperus sabina 'Tamariscifolia'

Rubus cockburnianus

Ground cover roses

Narcissus 'W.P. Milner'

Cotoneaster horizontalis

Rosa moyesii

Populus balsamifera (balsam poplar)

Narcissus 'February Silver'

Salix caprea (goat willow)

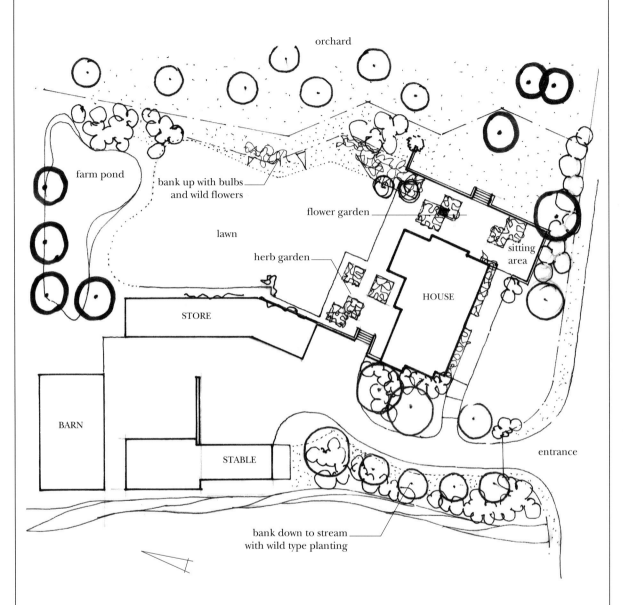

orchard

farm pond

bank up with bulbs
and wild flowers

flower garden

lawn

herb garden

sitting
area

STORE

HOUSE

BARN

STABLE

entrance

bank down to stream
with wild type planting

sheep, lambs and flowering plums are a major feature in spring – and the farm pond was cleared and slightly enlarged to give further interest to the north of the house. Spring- and summer-flowering yellow flag irises, white arum lilies, bullrushes and flats of marsh marigold are planted at the edge.

Wide gravel terraces surround the house and beds of herbs outside the kitchen above the yard change to flower gardens at the east end. Steps from the terrace lead to a lawned area where the evening sun can be enjoyed. The existing trees here include a good walnut.

Most people park in the yard and enter the house through the boot-room and a thick, semi-native planting of trees and shrubs attempts to shelter this entrance from the prevailing wind. The planting continues around the house to thicken the field hedge and give more privacy from the road.

A GARDEN IN WOODLAND

In this garden at the rear of a stone-built farm-house plantsman Dan Pearson has used simple plant material in a new and exciting way.

The house is on a south-facing fall at the end of a long lane, through gated fields. The garden is surrounded on two sides by trees and is terraced up from the north side of the house. It gets little sun in winter because of the house and surrounding trees. In summer, however, when the sun reaches the sheltered space, there are hidden retreats among its great masses of voluptuous planting. From the retreats – circles of

Below: Purple hazel (*Corylus avellana* 'Purpurea') frames a view backed by white poplar (*Populus alba*). In front is *Crambe cordifolia* with astrantia, lady's mantle (*Alchemilla*) and field geranium. The fern is *Dryopteris filix-mas*.

Right: The house and its garden are approached across gated meadows golden in spring with buttercups. New shelter planting protects the site from cold winds; where once a screen of Scots pine (*Pinus sylvestris*) stood, thorn, larch and field maple are visible along the boundary.

grass or brick-paved 'rooms' – the view over the garden and beyond the house is of rolling Northamptonshire fields.

The planting was designed to be wild in effect, heavy on form and to make a transition between domesticity and the surrounding mixed woodland. Herbs are combined with generous shrub drifts interspersed with perennials. This overwhelming mix is both casual and sophisticated. It is in the cottage garden tradition in its selection, but a successor to the Edwardian in its massed exuberance.

The planting in this terrace steps up to meet its wooded backdrop. Lovely bold masses of mixed foliage and flower contrast with bricks and gravel. Trailing from the left are elderflowers at the back of the border with broom (*Cytisus*) and *Iris foetidissima* in front. Then there is a gold-foliaged *Philadelphus coronarius* 'Aureus' with clouds of fluffy white *Crambe cordifolia* on its right. There is grey globe artichoke foliage, sedum and lavender in front, with purple sage (*Salvia purpurescens*), Russian sage (*Perovskia*), purple *Cotinus coggygria*, euphorbia and fuzzy purple fennel foliage. Used in this way the beauty of herb foliages really stands out. This is not a colourful border in the flower garden sense – but an essay in foliage usage. Flowers are the bonus.

AN ENCLOSED HERB GARDEN

The concept of a herb garden within sheltering walls is appealing, and this is just such a location. An older house was modernized and its area enclosed by a new wall and gateway. The court-yard – for this is what the area has now become – steps down to the house across broad areas of stone paving combined with masses of granite sett, of which there was a ready supply.

The east side of the courtyard, against the far wall from the house, is planted with mixed shrubs which run into shade-loving specimens and ferns beneath the fig tree and down the north-facing border. The herbs are mixed with the odd shrub rose and are both culinary – the kitchen looks into the garden – and decorative. This is an entrance area and first impressions do count.

Styling matters in such a location and house, wall, pavings and plantings should blend to create the correct ambience. Annuals, for colour, in half-barrels complete the 'mellowed out' look.

Herbs are excellent plants for their foliage effect alone, and in a small urban space the fact that they are evergreen, or evergrey, creates a fullness that will continue throughout winter.

If this is the style you seek to create, include

Above: Although the planting of this enclosed area is mainly of herbs, there are other shrubby subjects that like the same poor soil and hot, dry conditions. In the foreground is Jerusalem sage (*Phlomis fruticosa*) and beyond it a New Zealand daisy bush (*Olearia macrodonta*). To its left is purple sage (*Salvia purpurescens*) with chives (*Allium schoenoprasum*) and thyme. At the base of this bed is grey senecio with *Ozothamnus rosmarifolius*.

Left: Overall plan of the garden.

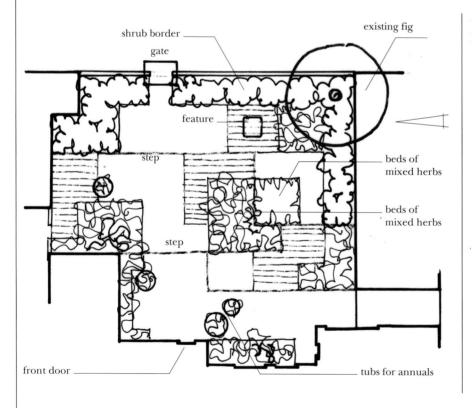

shrub border

gate

existing fig

feature

step

beds of mixed herbs

beds of mixed herbs

step

front door

tubs for annuals

Right: The random flooring of this enclosed space is of granite sett and slabs of old York stone. In the hottest position in the garden a mixture of culinary herbs nestles next to the Jerusalem sage. Much of the vegetation of this smallish space is evergreen and/or purple, which gives a fully furnished effect throughout the year.

decorative subjects such as rosemary and its many forms with lavender and perennial geraniums too. Mix less vigorous shrub roses, with regale lilies for fragrance. Cottage gardeners of the past also planted madonna lilies (*Lilium candidum*) but I find these difficult to establish.

For spring interest include simple tulips – the lily-flowered type are a favourite – followed by native Solomon's seal (*Polygonatum multiflorum*) and lily of the valley (*Convallaria majalis*) in moist shade. Try species gladioli too. Use iris where they will be hot enough, lupins and paeonies and anything daisy-ish including species aster. Monkshood (*Aconitum*) is an autumn favourite; its blue spikes last until they are cut down by frost.

In an enclosed town garden I would not be without the fragrance of tall white tobacco plants (*Nicotiana*) in late summer, combined with early and late forms of native honeysuckle (*Lonicera periclymenum* 'Belgica' and *L.p.* 'Serotina').

I do not feel that the formality of box edging is correct when creating a loose 'country' effect. It is a heritage of the Edwardian garden – without the Edwardian gardener to maintain it!

A GARDEN IN A FIELD

The owners of this newly converted barn and outbuildings were not seeking a decorative garden as such. Rather, they wanted a setting for the house and a layout and plantings to fulfil specific objectives.

The first of these was to shelter the site, which is an open, windswept field, without losing its excellent views over rolling Wiltshire downland. The barn is on an east-west axis and strong prevailing winds come from the south-west.

The second objective, and indeed the reason the owners moved to the barn, was to keep goats on their land. A system of secure fields and grazing was therefore a necessary element in the design of the garden.

Both objectives were fulfilled by the creation of a ha-ha ditch of concrete-block walling around one side of the mown lawn areas to keep the goats out and provide an uninterrupted view. The surplus earth that became available was used to raise the ground level against the substantial stone wall that encloses the barn forecourt. Shelter planting on this mound instantly nestles the building into its site.

When moving earth – a digger can do this in a little over a day in dry weather – set all topsoil to one side, correct the levels in the subsoil and then replace the topsoil. Do not sandwich a mixed layer of top and subsoil. Topsoil is rich in organic matter and is the normal growing medium; subsoil is not.

The shelter plants are Austrian pine (*Pinus nigra austriaca*), which branches to the ground, mixed with field maples (*Acer campestre*) and shrub roses. The pines are fairly slow-growing, but height is not of primary importance. The field maples will move fast but can be pollarded back eventually and thinned as the pines grow up. A grove of tough walnut trees was planted within the consolidated gravel forecourt to increase protection from the wind.

An area to the north of the barn, between it and an old cart shed, is ideal for growing vegetables and herbs. A path round the 'garden' side of the house connects this area with the stone terrace. An existing small field-pond that will be opened out to encourage further wildlife is the culmination of the garden part of the layout.

This interaction of practical activity with decorative surroundings and household requirements may well be the way forward for anyone fortunate enough to own a field or fields. Disused country buildings are being sensitively restored and their surroundings should not suburbanize the countryside in which they sit. Plantings and layouts must reflect a former age and usage, but also be practical for today.

Plan showing how shelter plants are positioned to protect the house and converted barn from the strong south-westerly winds that blow up the entrance drive. The small herb and vegetable garden is clustered at the other end of the house where it is sheltered among old outbuildings.

The east aspect of the barn looks out over a terrace to a lawn and downland. To the south, across a ha-ha ditch, there is a view towards proposed livestock.

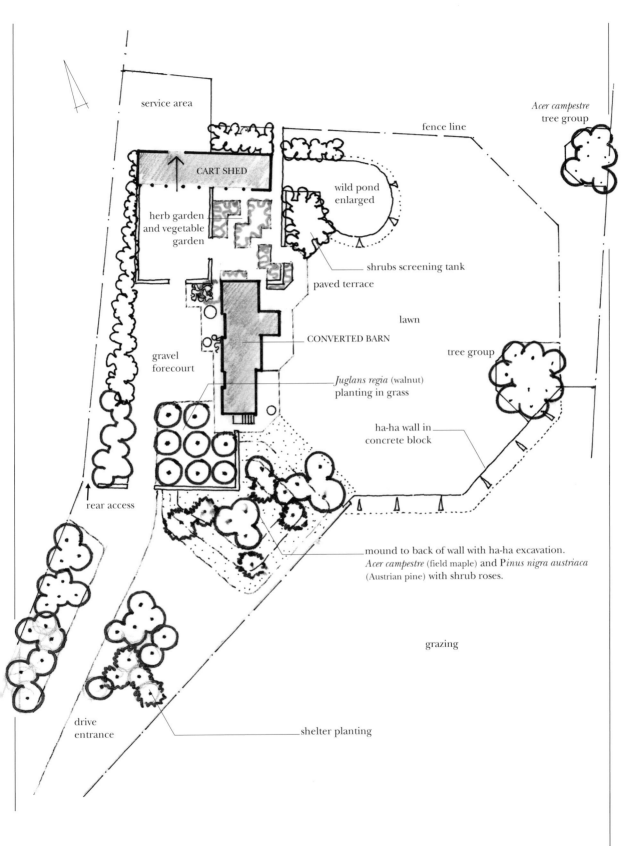

service area

fence line

Acer campestre
tree group

CART SHED

herb garden
and vegetable
garden

wild pond
enlarged

shrubs screening tank

paved terrace

lawn

gravel
forecourt

CONVERTED BARN

Juglans regia (walnut)
planting in grass

tree group

ha-ha wall in
concrete block

rear access

mound to back of wall with ha-ha excavation.
Acer campestre (field maple) and P*inus nigra austriaca*
(Austrian pine) with shrub roses.

grazing

drive
entrance

shelter planting

A GARDEN ON CHALK DOWNLAND

A sheep-fold high on chalk downs has been made into a house with a guest apartment, garage, central courtyard garden and storage space. Shepherds originally lived here with their sheep during the all-important lambing time.

Strict planning controls ensured that when the building was converted the dark-stained boarding on its side remained. The horse chestnut which is the fulcrum of the garden was built into the layout to overcome the scale of the building. A large box tree or yew would have been more locally correct, but difficult to locate to any size.

Cars come into the sheep-fold and park to the left. The entrance to the house is up bold, wide steps to the left of the chestnut. There are three punctuating sitting-places. The first has a built-in stone table outside the front door. This corner gets the morning sun and has a view across the hard gravelled yard to the downland beyond. The second space, for the sun at noon, adjoins the main barn. The space for afternoons and summer evenings is by the open sheep-fold opposite the house.

The layout of the garden, along with its planting, follows the sun.

There was initially a conflict of interest in selecting plants for this exposed chalky site. The designer preferred what was known to be tough. The client, with a love of Provence, sought something more exotic. A balance has been

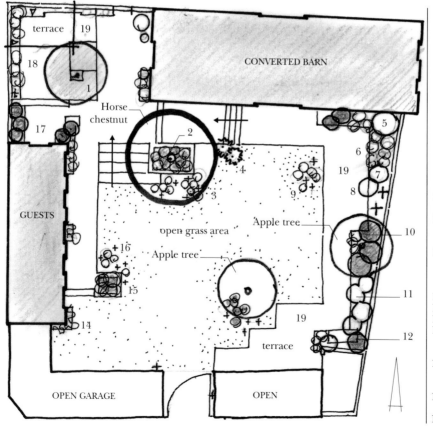

1. *Arbutus andrachne* (strawberry tree)
2. *Santolina incana* (cotton lavender)
3. *Kniphofia caulescens* with *Alchemilla mollis* (lady's mantle)
4. *Euphorbia wulfenii* (spurge)
5. Figure with *Rosa* 'Mermaid' and *Choisya ternata* (Mexican orange blossom)
6. *Phlomis fruticosa* (Jerusalem sage)
7. *Perovskia atriplicifolia*
8. White *Buddleia davidii*
9. Iris with *Alchemilla mollis* (lady's mantle)
10. *Elaeagnus x ebbingei* with *Bergenia stracheyi* 'Silberlicht'
11. *Cynara scolymus* (globe artichoke) with *Crambe cordifolia*
12. *Rhus typhina* (stag's horn sumach), *Taxus baccata* 'Fastigiata' (Irish yew) and *Hydrangea arborescens*
13. *Iris foetidissima* (gladdon)
14. *Garrya eliptica*
15. *Cistus x corbariensis*
16. *Helleborus corsicus* (winter helebore) with *Alchemilla mollis* (lady's mantle)
17. *Euonymus ovatus*, *Pyracantha rogersiana* and *Iris foetidissima* (gladdon)
18. Climbing roses with *Vitis coignetiae*
19. Sitting places

Right: On the left is the guest accommodation with, beyond the sitting corner, the house/barn. The guest house is built of flint, the local building material; vines will grow up the oak pergola in summer.

Hellebore (*Helleborus corsicus*) and *Sisyrinchium striatum* seed into the foreground gravel surfacing to the central space. Cistus grows above the lefthand retaining wall.

A strawberry tree (*Arbutus unedo*) is planted in front of the pergola.

Below left: From the main barn conversion the view is across a gravelled central space. The paved area provides shelter from the wind.

The tree in the pot is an olive which spends the winter months under cover.

Below: Bold, simple masses of decorative perennial material do not distract from the superb downland view beyond the garden.

achieved between the two. Grass as well as a ground cover was considered, but seemed too soft for such a structured enclosure. Two older apple trees were included to provide a domestic feeling – the client would have preferred olives!

In the gravel beneath the trees, and at edges that cannot be reached by cars, masses of irises are planted with other self-seeding biennials, verbascum, alchemilla, sisyrinchium and, in the shade, hellebore (*Helleborus foetidus*). The manner of their planting – strewn through the gravel base – is probably of more interest than the plants themselves. The major plantings are not exotic and steady the prettier material growing beneath them.

A unity between building and site was created by using hard materials in sympathy with the local flint and brick.

A GARDEN ON EXPOSED DOWNLAND

The owners of this bungalow perched high on the Hampshire downs enjoy a breathtaking view, but the site is exposed to the winter winds and there is little sense of enclosure: afforestation falls away from the house on its south side and there is a meagre planting between it and a country road on the east and west and hedgerow on its northern boundary.

The first tasks were to create an entrance to the bungalow and terraces to surround the house and link the interior with the exterior, then to plant the terraces to create intimate spaces. Plant selection was restricted to subjects that will grow on a more or less solid chalk soil with maximum exposure to the wind.

The terrace planting includes pine (*Pinus mugo*), low-growing juniper (*Juniperus communis*), barberry, (*Berberis thunbergii*) and potentilla masses. Foliage variation against the dark brick of the terraces is provided by grey lavender (*Lavandula officinalis*) and senecio 'Sunshine' with euonymus 'Emerald 'n Gold'. Mixed with these are herbs such as thyme, sage, angelica and rosemary which do well in this bright, well-drained location. Perennial masses of Shasta daisies (*Chrysanthemum maximum*) and irises come through the shrubs and there are plenty of evergreens for winter enclosure. Most of these plants are natives and all are tough and easy to look after.

To the north of the house there is a longer term planting of trees with, through them, a manageable mowing pattern. Much of the grass remains rough, needing mowing only a few times per year, but it makes sense for the rides to be mowable. The broad, curving pattern of rough grass with mown is easily negotiable with a sit-on mower.

Spring and autumn bulbs are encouraged in the rough grass, with wild flowers which continue to grow to the height of the mower's cut – for a chalk meadow is rich with flowers. When flower heads are removed by the mower they do not make seed and therefore do not regenerate.

Wild flowers are not particularly easy to create artificially or sustain. One method is to remove the existing grass shard and re-seed it with a wild flower and grass seed mix appropriate for the particular location (this is vital). The selected grasses will not be as invasive as the wild ones and will allow the flower seeds to germinate and flourish. Eventually, however, wild grasses will invade again and dominate.

Another method is to plant out pot-grown seedlings of wild flowers among an established sward – a time-consuming exercise.

I believe that by sustaining a regular high mow you will eventually get a range of wild flowers that grow to that height naturally, and this is the practice in this location.

The existing boundary hedge on the north was thorn, hazel and field maple. This is now supplemented with holly (*Ilex aquifolium*), viburnum (*V. opulus*) and yew (*Taxus baccata*) masses encroaching into the garden, and hornbeam (*Carpinus betulus*), wild white cherry (*Prunus avium* 'Plena') and whitebeam (*Sorbus aria* 'Lutescens'). Red oaks (*Quercus rubra*) have also been planted with flowering thorn (*Crataegus prunifolia*) and crab apple *Malus* 'Golden Hornet' nearer the house.

On either side of the drive entrance to the house there is a long-term planting of trees and shrubs which will sit amongst areas of rough grass. Broad swathes can be mown through the grass to create a pattern.

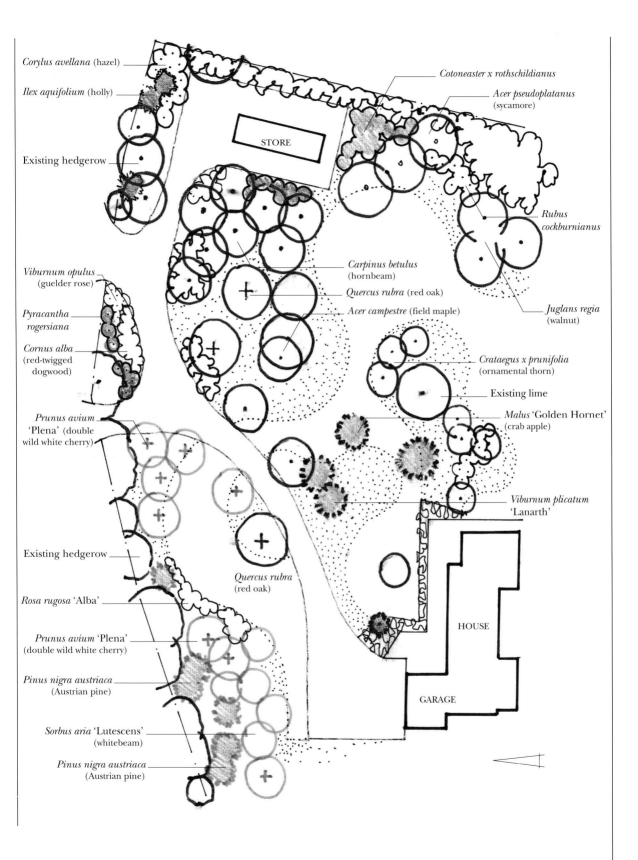

Corylus avellana (hazel)

Ilex aquifolium (holly)

Existing hedgerow

Cotoneaster x rothschildianus

Acer pseudoplatanus
(sycamore)

STORE

Rubus
cockburnianus

Viburnum opulus
(guelder rose)

Pyracantha
rogersiana

Cornus alba
(red-twigged
dogwood)

Carpinus betulus
(hornbeam)

Quercus rubra (red oak)

Acer campestre (field maple)

Juglans regia
(walnut)

Crataegus x prunifolia
(ornamental thorn)

Existing lime

Malus 'Golden Hornet'
(crab apple)

Prunus avium
'Plena' (double
wild white cherry)

Viburnum plicatum
'Lanarth'

Existing hedgerow

Rosa rugosa 'Alba'

Prunus avium 'Plena'
(double wild white cherry)

Pinus nigra austriaca
(Austrian pine)

Sorbus aria 'Lutescens'
(whitebeam)

Pinus nigra austriaca
(Austrian pine)

Quercus rubra
(red oak)

HOUSE

GARAGE

A GARDEN BELOW DOWNLAND

This fifty-year-old garden was originally created by Joyce Robinson, a great plantswoman. She laid out and planted its bones and I have subsequently been experimenting here to extend her natural look. The garden is at the foot of chalk downs where the soil is poor and gravelly, but its own soil is practically neutral.

In the part of the garden where the layout is seen against a field, Joyce Robinson planted wild-looking subjects that did not contrast with the pastoral. At the same time they had a flavour of the damp since this is the lowest level of the garden. She also created a dry gravel stream running towards the area. It is this sound, underlying philosophy that I took over and sought to extend.

The bones of the planting are made up of an unlikely redwood (*Sequoia sempervirens*) with a

Above: A snake-barked maple (*Acer pensylvanicum*) marks the end of the gravel before it runs into a large pond. Beyond are areas of rough grass with *Narcissus* 'W.P. Milner'.

Right: A dry gravel stream runs towards water. There are primroses (*Primula vulgaris*) in the 'stream' and blue *Brunnera macrophylla* at its edge.

koelreuteria (*K. paniculata*). There are two self-seeded silver birches (*Betula pendula*) and, beneath them, a mass of bamboo – *Arundinaria fastuosa* and *A. variegata* – against whose feathery backdrop in winter the red stems of red-twigged dogwood (*Cornus alba*) and the yellow ones of the white willow (*Salix alba* 'Vitellina') shine out. White-stemmed rubus (*Rubus cockburnianus*) and black willow (*Salix fargesii*) complete the winter look.

In early spring there are primroses in the gravel, forget-me-nots, and bright blue drifts of brunnera (*B. macrophylla*) beneath the silver birch contrasting with groups of violas (*Viola labradorica*).

Clumps of angelica come next – it is another

Right: In late spring buttercups take over from spring bulbs in areas of rough grass (which incidentally reduces maintenance of the garden area). Almost hidden among the buttercups are masses of speedwell (*Veronica officinalis*) on the right with bugle (*Ajuga reptans*).

self-seeder – with the cream flowers of viburnum (*V. plicatum* 'Mariesii'). They are followed by masses of naturalized-looking lupins (I replant them every two or three years) growing with emergent lady's mantle (*Alchemilla mollis*). Slowly the leaves of the dogwood and willows come out, with snowberry (*Symphoricarpos*) and elder (*Sambucus nigra*). Masses of foxgloves (*Digitalis purpurea*) grow between them. By summer the grasses – fluffy *Deschampsia caespitosa* and *Miscanthus* – contrast well with good evergreen

Above: Few shrubs have as strong a horizontal line as this *Viburnum plicatum* 'Mariesii'. It also has good foliage colour in autumn. To maintain the horizontal effect, prune out the strong vertical leader growths each year.

Below: A plan of a wild area at the bottom of the garden. Through it runs a loose gravel path leading to a natural pool beyond. The gravel medium allows a loose planting in the path.

Right: The central gravel path through the planting has *Miscanthus* grass emerging on the left. On the right is a twisted form of our native hazel, *Corylus avellana* 'Contorta', with foxgloves (*Digitalis* *purpurea*), verbascum, lady's mantle (*Alchemilla mollis*) and forget-me-nots in the foreground. The grasses on the right are seedling tufted hair grass (*Deschampsia caespitosa*).

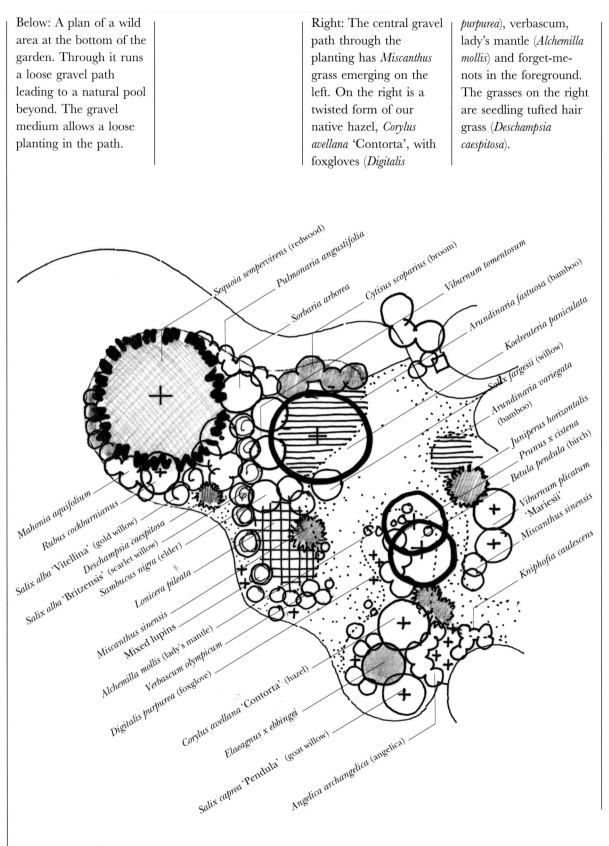

Sequoia sempervirens (redwood)
Pulmonaria angustifolia
Sorbaria arborea
Cytisus scoparius (broom)
Viburnum tomentosum
Arundinaria fastuosa (bamboo)
Koelreuteria paniculata
Salix fargesii (willow)
Arundinaria variegata (bamboo)
Juniperus horizontalis
Prunus x cistena
Betula pendula (birch)
Viburnum plicatum 'Mariesii'
Miscanthus sinensis
Kniphofia caulescens

Mahonia aquifolium
Rubus cockburnianus
Salix alba 'Vitellina' (gold willow)
Deschampsia caespitosa
Salix alba 'Britzensis' (scarlet willow)
Sambucus nigra (elder)
Lonicera pileata
Miscanthus sinensis
Mixed lupins
Alchemilla mollis (lady's mantle)
Verbascum olympicum
Digitalis purpurea (foxglove)
Corylus avellana 'Contorta' (hazel)
Elaeagnus x ebbingei
Salix caprea 'Pendula' (goat willow)
Angelica archangelica (angelica)

Kniphofia caulescens. The twisted shapes of *Corylus avellana* 'Contorta' stems become apparent as the leaves drop, as do the showering stems of goat willow (*Salix caprea*) which later carry pussy-willow-type flowers.

This is not a total planting of natives, but a mixture of their hybridized forms and introduced species. The freedom of the gravel ground cover,

Above: On sharp, bright days of winter the one-year wood of certain *Cornus* and *Salix* species makes a bright splash of colour. This planting is of *Salix alba* 'Vitellina' with *S.a.* 'Britzensis'.

Right: Through the catkins of a shrubby pussy willow (*Salix caprea*) the outline of the pool sweeps round. In the foreground are the new leaves of *Iris pseudacorus*.

which allows for a random placement, is what really creates the wild look.

Curiously enough, wilder types of planting need severe thinning and pruning. Nature's groupings thin themselves naturally in the process of achieving the climax vegetation of their area and the gardener must seek to maintain a balance between the layers of plants. Many natural plantings seem to be lighter and more graceful than those of the Edwardian border, for what is being asked of them is different: one is for real and the other is highly artificial. I have tried to marry the concepts.

A GARDEN ON URBAN CLAY

This town garden, built on clay, is very small, walled and at the rear of an Edwardian terrace house. All access is through the house. The garden was built at the same time as a conservatory off the kitchen and identical tiled flooring is used both inside and outside on the small terrace.

It is a garden to be seen rather than used, and its layout is a compromise between structure and planting. The latter was to be decorative, but also functional in that it extends the basic design concept from within and screens where necessary outside. Gardens like this are always seen against the rear of other people's houses and what they have planted. It's called 'the view'.

A single, small tree, the 'special', makes a visual transition from inside to outside and vice versa and works proportionally with the sundial. The brick pattern holds the eye in the site. Loose, natural planting in consolidated gravel softens the effect. Gravel is cheap, it allows random planting and avoids the surrounding border approach. It must be hard and consolidated if it is not to be used by cats.

Native yew (*Taxus baccata*) provides a dark skeleton for the layout. On the right a yew hedge

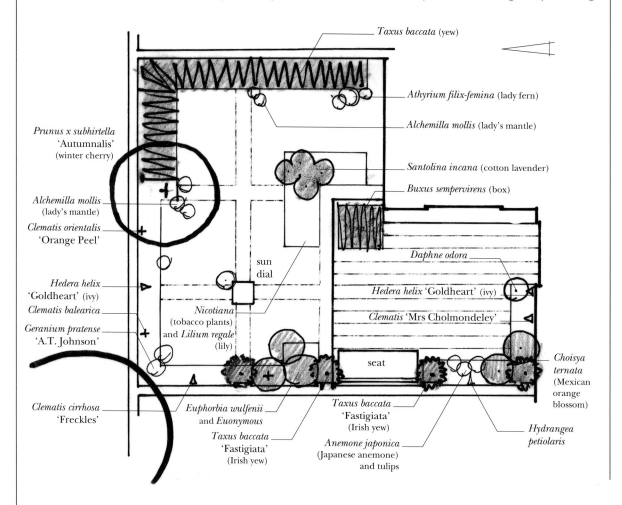

Taxus baccata (yew)

Athyrium filix-femina (lady fern)

Alchemilla mollis (lady's mantle)

Prunus x subhirtella 'Autumnalis' (winter cherry)

Santolina incana (cotton lavender)

Buxus sempervirens (box)

Alchemilla mollis (lady's mantle)

Clematis orientalis 'Orange Peel'

Daphne odora

sun dial

Hedera helix 'Goldheart' (ivy)

Hedera helix 'Goldheart' (ivy)

Clematis balearica

Clematis 'Mrs Cholmondeley'

Geranium pratense 'A.T. Johnson'

Nicotiana (tobacco plants) and *Lilium regale* (lily)

seat

Choisya ternata (Mexican orange blossom)

Clematis cirrhosa 'Freckles'

Euphorbia wulfenii and *Euonymous*

Taxus baccata 'Fastigiata' (Irish yew)

Hydrangea petiolaris

Taxus baccata 'Fastigiata' (Irish yew)

Anemone japonica (Japanese anemone) and tulips

screens the party wall and links the small tree back to the house. On the left, upright or Irish yews (*Taxus baccata* 'Fastigiata') repeat the dark green and echo the wall buttresses behind them. Other structural plants include euphorbia (*E. wulfenii*) with a euonymous behind it, Mexican orange (*Choisya ternata* cotton lavender (*Santolina incana*) and box (*Buxus sempervirens*).

The garden faces due north and will always be a green bower rather than a flowery one. But perennial geraniums (*G. pratense* 'A. T. Johnson') will provide spring colour, with green-flowering lady's mantle (*Alchemilla mollis*) growing loosely in the gravel in summer, followed by late-flowering white Japanese anemones (*A. japonica*). Annual plantings of white tobacco flowers (*Nicotiana*) and lilies (*Lilium regale*) supply fragrance.

Above: *Hedera helix* 'Goldheart' – a popular small-leafed ivy – can brighten dark urban walls with bright splashes of gold upon an otherwise green leaf. A good foil to alchemilla!

Right: Lady's mantle (*Alchemilla mollis*) prefers light shade, but will in fact grow anywhere. A great self-seeder, it has velvety rounded leaves that catch the dew, and foaming lime-green flowers in June and July.

Left: Plan of a small urban space with loose planting, mainly in shade.

A GARDEN ON MOORLAND

Everyone's concept of a garden is very different. To many people it means colour. It is fantasy to others or peace and escape from the outside world. I seek tranquillity and a sense of fitness for location.

Of all the gardens I know, one of the most tranquil – throughout the year – is high up on windswept Dartmoor. It is a horticulturist's

Above: Above a treed valley in central Dartmoor this garden receives the full blast of south-westerly winds and a very high rainfall. In the summer season sculptures are displayed for public enjoyment.

Right: A series of semi-wild pools descends down the garden, which is planted almost exclusively with a wide range of birches underplanted with moss and bilberry (*Vaccinium myrtillus*). The birch on the left is *Betula pendula* 'Purpurea'.

Silver birch plantings on an exposed hillside on Dartmoor. The trees have been grouped to observe their growth pattern. There is a lesson in simplicity here, for even in early spring before the leaves appear there is a beauty in the multi-stemmed effect that they create.

The paths of mown grass lead the eye to the cultivated moorland that surrounds the site so that the garden is very much a part of its landscape.

garden in the sense that it is essentially a garden of trees that are suited to its site rather than one of high horticultural maintenance. Although the owner does not set out to be a garden designer, his sympathetic treatment of the sloping site is acutely sensitive to its location.

Kenneth Ashburner collects trees from habitats similar to this garden during his travels around the world. He often grows them from seed and then plants them as loose copses to observe their growth pattern. Grass grows roughly beneath the trees with patches of native heather, acid-loving

Left: A gentle bank runs down to a stream that flows through the site, ending in a pool at the bottom of the garden. In the boggy area at the top of the stream yellow flag iris (*Iris pseudacorus*) grow. Their pale green leaves are just showing with a patch of primrose (*Primula vulgaris*) beyond. The floor of this birch copse is a mossy bark mulch, with the leaves of ageing winter hellebore (*Helleborus corsicus*) masses.

Left: One of the summer sculptural exhibits provides a focal point through the craggy stems of river birch (*Betula nigra*) – an American form. The birch are planted on an island at the centre of the bottom pond.

vaccinium and wild roses. Wild flowers grow where they choose. Where necessary, paths are mown to encourage a view out to the surrounding swell of cultivated moorland.

June Ashburner sponsors a sculpture exhibition within the garden every summer and the contrast of objects with view and sympathetic planting is tranquil in the extreme. It is a lesson in the use of plant form contrasted with contour.

A TRADITIONAL HERB GARDEN

Surrounded by coppiced sweet chestnut (*Castanea sativa*) woodland on Wealden clay, this herb garden has stunning views over rolling southern countryside. It is the kind of little garden that must have existed for centuries for its layout is quartered – an early concept – and focuses on a central feature. But while the layout is balanced, its herbal planting softens the overall effect and the discipline of the layout supports the abandon

Above: The house is a traditional tile-hung Sussex farmhouse, originally approached up an oak-lined drive. The herb garden is on the right. The far shrub rose is 'Buff Beauty', a favourite.

Right: The herb garden is laid out in the traditional manner, with a central bird bath feature. Beyond the herb beds is another planted solely with the white shrub rose 'Blanc Double de Coubert'.

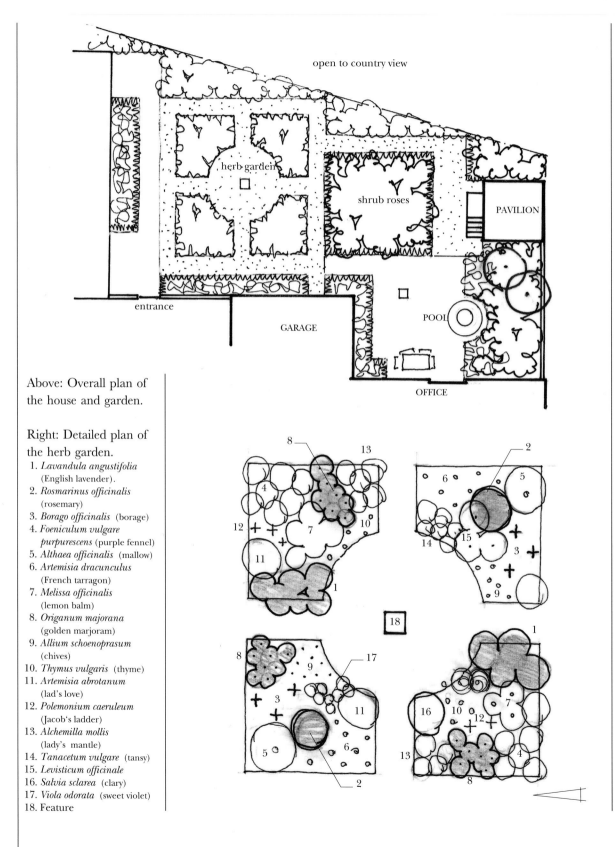

open to country view

herb garden

shrub roses

PAVILION

entrance

GARAGE

POOL

OFFICE

Above: Overall plan of
the house and garden.

Right: Detailed plan of
the herb garden.

1. *Lavandula angustifolia*
   (English lavender).
2. *Rosmarinus officinalis*
   (rosemary)
3. *Borago officinalis* (borage)
4. *Foeniculum vulgare*
   purpurescens (purple fennel)
5. *Althaea officinalis* (mallow)
6. *Artemisia dracunculus*
   (French tarragon)
7. *Melissa officinalis*
   (lemon balm)
8. *Origanum majorana*
   (golden marjoram)
9. *Allium schoenoprasum*
   (chives)
10. *Thymus vulgaris* (thyme)
11. *Artemisia abrotanum*
    (lad's love)
12. *Polemonium caeruleum*
    (Jacob's ladder)
13. *Alchemilla mollis*
    (lady's mantle)
14. *Tanacetum vulgare* (tansy)
15. *Levisticum officinale*
16. *Salvia sclarea* (clary)
17. *Viola odorata* (sweet violet)
18. Feature

of its planting. Herbs create this full and wild effect, which mirrors so well the way our native plants – many of which are herbs – grow.

Many herbs can stand exposure and wind. What they dislike is wet feet. A clay soil therefore needs lightening and opening up with gravel to improve its drainage. Organic matter makes the ground too rich – herbs thrive on deprivation.

Many herbs are evergreen. Rosemary, lavender and sage, which originate in the Mediterranean, prefer full sun. The smaller-leaved herbs like thyme are natives. The joy of all of them is their diversity of foliage form; their flowers are a bonus.

The herbs in this pretty layout are grown both for the kitchen and for decorative effect. It is a quiet and evocative garden which sits well within its woodland landscape; its plants are truly of their place.

Below: Beyond the boundary is a newly cut hayfield; inside the garden there is a mass of pink-flowering *Polygonum bistorta* with rosemary. Flowering chives (*Allium schoenoprasum*) are on the right.

Above: A hedge of *Cistus × corbariensis* contains the garden. The herbs include purple fennel (*Foeniculum vulgare purpurescens*), balm (*Melissa officinalis*), lavender (*Lavandula angustifolia*), thyme (*Thymus vulgaris*), violas (*Viola odorata*) and lady's mantle (*Alchemilla mollis*) with circular heads of flowering chives (*Allium schoenoprasum*).

A GARDEN IN THE NORTH

The garden of this red-brick terrace house outside Glasgow is north-facing and on acid soil. A new extension at the rear of the building has divided what is left of the garden almost in two, leaving a long, thin space enclosed by an immaculate privet hedge on the right and a high, coniferous hedge along the bottom. Tall beech trees in the neighbouring gardens provide a backdrop.

The existing planting was old rhododendrons that do well in shade and acid soil, and a motley collection of other garden centre 'goodies': a weeping cherry, some dwarf conifers and the occasional clump of heather.

The owners enjoy their garden and wanted somewhere to sit in the sun at weekends, and an area near the house for entertaining on summer evenings. Their dog requested some grass.

The interior of the house is crisp and bright, and the dining-room, which has a view down the length of the site, has a dark tiled floor and white furniture. This clean-cut use of colour and form decided the garden shape, structure and subsequent planting.

Much of the planting had to be evergreen as year-round interest was necessary to soften the geometry of the plan and connect the proportions of the garden with those of the surrounding hedges and the trees beyond them. In fact, there is much silver and grey 'evergreen' foliage; the garden was the owners' present to themselves on a significant anniversary.

Yew (*Taxus baccata* 'Fastigiata') and euonymous (*E. fortunei* 'Silver Queen' and *E. ovatus*) provide the bones of the layout, with buddleias (*B. davidii*), hardy fuchsias (*F. magellanica*) and rosemary for the more colourful and exotic shrubby infill. Perennials include irises, lupins, monkshood, sedum (*S. spectabile*), winter hellebores (*Helleborus corsicus*) and lilies of the valley (*Convallaria majalis*).

All are tough and well-tried favourites for what is not the easiest climate or location.

The culmination of the garden is a summerhouse couched in vegetation. The path down the righthand side of the garden acts as an edging to planting that will eventually sprawl over it.

Plan showing the type of wilder planting, though of mainly garden varieties, which can be used to plant up a town garden. The plan is inward looking, focusing on the silver birch group, though the view from the house is directed towards a new summer house and neighbouring beech tree.

1. *Hedera helix* 'Goldheart'
2. *Lavandula vera* (lavender)
3. *Helleborus corsicus* (winter hellebore) and *Convallaria majalis* (lily of the valley)
4. *Senecio laxifolius*
5. *Taxus baccata* 'Fastigiata' (Irish yew)
6. Clipped yew
7. *Euonymus fortunei* 'Silver Queen'
8. *Ceratostigma willmottianum*
9. *Helleborus corsicus* (winter hellebore) and *Anemone japonica*
10. *Bergenia stracheyi* 'Silberlicht'
11. *Anemone japonica* 'Alba'
12. *Chaenomeles speciosa* 'Kermesina Semi-Plena'
13. 3 *Betula pendula* (birch)
14. *Fatsia japonica*
15. Existing philadelphus
16. *Fuchsia magellanica*
17. Existing rhododendron
18. Existing weeping cherry
19. Tall beech hedge.
20. *Mahonia japonica*
21. *Helleborus corsicus* (winter hellebore)
22. Existing philadelphus
23. *Macleaya cordata*
24. Existing berberis
25. *Rhus typhina* 'Laciniata' (Stag's horn)
26. *Ligustrum ovalifolium* 'Argenteum' (privet)
27. Large beech tree next door
28. *Prunus subhirtella* 'Autumnalis' (cherry)
29. *Rosmarinus officinalis* 'Fastigiata' (rosemary upright)
30. *Potentilla fruticosa* 'Mandschurica'
31. Miscanthus sinensis
32. *Buddleia davidii* 'White Cloud'
33. Euonymus ovatus
34. Iris
35. *Fuchsia magellanica* 'Variegata'
36. Lupin
37. *Lavandula spica* 'Hidcote' (lavender)
38. *Sedum spectabile* 'Autumn Joy'
39. *Euonymus fortunei* 'Silver Queen', clipped
40. Privet hedge
41. *Taxus baccata* 'Fastigiata' (Irish yew)

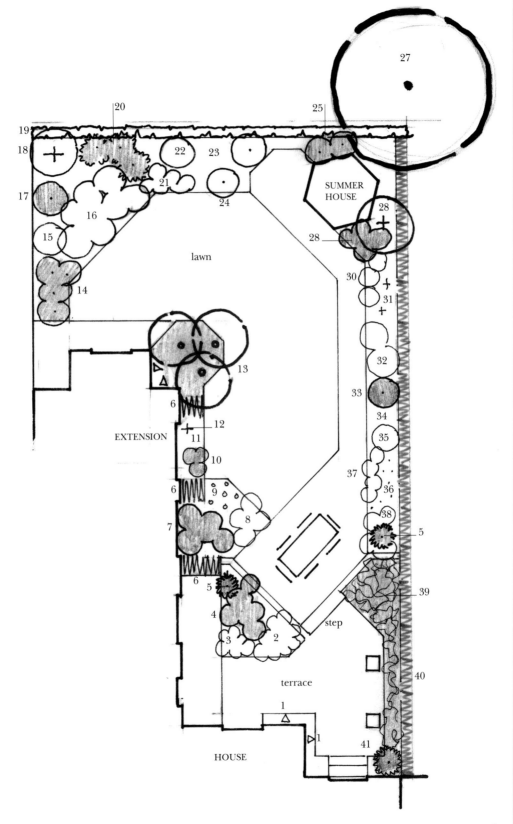

20

19
18

17

15

14

16

22   23

21

24

lawn

25

SUMMER
HOUSE

28

28

27

30

31

32

33

34

35

37

36

38

5

13

EXTENSION

12

11

10

9

8

6

6

7

6

5

4

3   2

step

1

1

terrace

HOUSE

41

39

40

A GARDEN WITHIN A GARDEN

Travelling in Italy you sometimes come to an exotic little corner in a larger garden. It smells of box and heat and you think that is what the real Tuscany is all about. This garden has the same feel. It is walled and enclosed, but surrounded by large trees – and the birds that

Right: A small flower border beneath a native whitebeam (*Sorbus aria*) lies on the other side of the avenue. Through it runs a metal pergola over which is growing a golden form of the native hop (*Humulus lupulus* 'Aureus').

inhabit them. Increasingly I think that the sound of birds adds hugely to a garden's magic.

It is the inner sanctum of a larger garden. The outer part has a small, formal avenue of lime trees (*Tilea × euchlora*) linking the house to a view of rolling countryside. Off to one side is a small flower garden and to the other a newly planted plan of the old house which was destroyed by fire. It's a lovely idea, but needing time to establish.

Through the house and a stone-floored kitchen you come to the walled garden.

Unlike some ideal gardens, which can be daunting because they are so conscious of themselves,

Above: An avenue of lime trees links the house to the country view. The unmown daisy lawn provides an attractive ground cover! Beyond the trees boxwood hedges are starting to form the old house plan.

this one just happened, one feels, and if it is a bit 'weedy' it is enchanting and a place in which to relax. Its charm is hard to define.

There is its ambience, of course, and good planting and practicality. But there is a touch of something else: the feeling that things could be getting away from its owners – and their cats. (Gertrude Jekyll had a thing about cats in her gardens; they provide a peaceful accompaniment.)

Below: A plan of the walled garden entered from the house on the bottom right. A new conservatory/greenhouse dominates the layout which, though semi-formal, contains a mass of cottage plantings.

Right: The path running down the centre of the conservatory is edged on the foreground with box (*Buxus sempervirens*) and then chives (*Allium schoenoprasum*). Beyond is a mass of blue aquilegia, with on the right violas and beyond them the poached egg plant (*Limnanthes douglasii*) and white arabis.

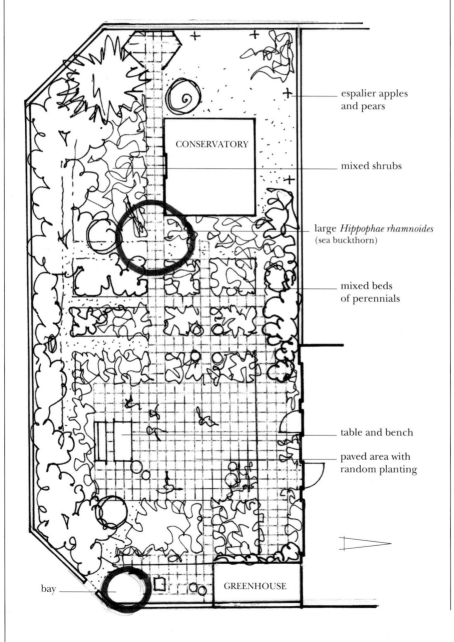

CONSERVATORY

espalier apples
and pears

mixed shrubs

large *Hippophae rhamnoides*
(sea buckthorn)

mixed beds
of perennials

table and bench

paved area with
random planting

bay

GREENHOUSE

Below: At the edge of the outer garden rhubarb flowers provide an interesting foil to sycamore and oak clumps in the meadow beyond.

Since I first visited this garden the owners have added a 6 m (20 ft) square conservatory – really a greenhouse. This structure is now the focal point of the garden, and where a standard sea buckthorn (*Hippophae rhamnoides*) was once the feature, it now complements the conservatory. In front of them are a series of small 'medieval' beds bursting with perennials: good, old-fashioned aquilegias and paeonies, pinks and iris, lots of herbs, violas and allium heads about to burst.

The garden leads out from a huge farmhouse kitchen, the hub of the action in this household, and there is a central paved area with, as its main feature, a large marble table with a bench behind it.

This small corner – of town garden dimensions – may be only part of a larger garden, but it is a very special place.

Above: The new
conservatory in the
centre of the garden is
framed by a good-sized
specimen of sea
buckthorn (*Hippophae
rhamnoides*), which makes
a good, craggy, small
grey tree. Beyond the
wall is a neighbouring
traditional dovecote. In
May the garden is
studded with masses of
aquilegia of mixed
colours with grey lamb's
ear (*Stachys lanata*) in the
foreground.

A GARDEN IN A VALLEY

This barn lies at the bottom of a valley and stands between two large oaks in a sheltered hollow at the corner of a field – a rough piece of ground with very wet, acid clay soil.

The original approach to it was up a track by a field hedge, but when the barn was converted the drive was given a wide loop and fitted into the swelling contours of a large field above the house. The enlarged garden within this loop was to remain fieldlike, and adjoining plantings were to be wild in character.

At the front of the house the forecourt looked down to a large field pond. It was quite a feature, but problems with neighbours meant that it could not be even a borrowed part of the setting. For the same reason, the old run of thorn and holly hedge at the rear of the house which obstructed a good field view could not be adjusted. Terrace shapes and levels therefore direct the view inwards to the oaks rather than outwards to the landscape.

The new tree planting along the drive is of balsam poplar (*Populus balsamifera*) for the spring smell of its young foliage, with *Malus floribunda*, a free-flowering white crab apple that is only one up on *M. sylvestris*, our native crab apple. There are two bird cherries (*Prunus padus*) against the black boarding of the barn itself.

Shrubs are seen against the backdrop of the countryside – and also hide the septic tank. The planting is of holly (*Ilex aquifolium*) with hazel (*Corylus avellana*), laurustinus (*Viburnum tinus*), goat willow or pussy willow (*Salix caprea*) and red-twigged dogwood (*Cornus alba*) and yellow-stemmed willow (*Salix alba* 'Vitellina'). Both are kept stooled down. White-stemmed *Rubus cockburnianus* grows through white-flowering *Viburnum plicatum* 'Lanarth', backed by a stand of tall pampas grass which bends into the pond.

On the pond-side a species rose (*Rosa moyesii*) with lacy foliage and flagon-shaped hips combines with the sweet-smelling foliage of our native sweet

Below: Plan showing the native shrubs around and near the septic tank.

Right: Overall plan showing how the garden surrounds the barn.

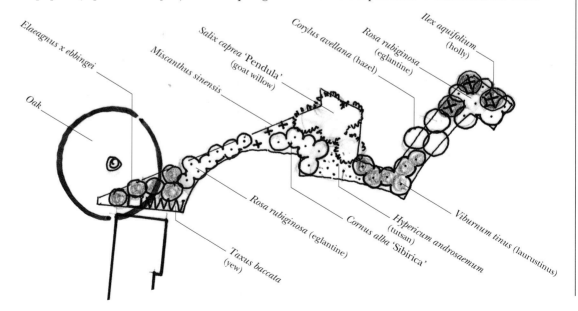

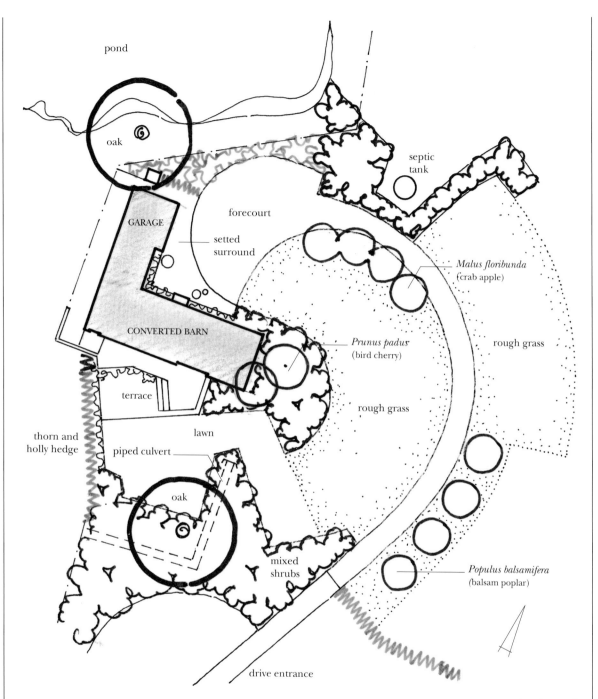

pond

oak

septic
tank

GARAGE

forecourt

setted
surround

Malus floribunda
(crab apple)

CONVERTED BARN

Prunus padus
(bird cherry)

rough grass

terrace

rough grass

thorn and
holly hedge

lawn

piped culvert

oak

mixed
shrubs

Populus balsamifera
(balsam poplar)

drive entrance

briar (*Rosa rubiginosa*). At the end is a clump of grey elaeagnus (*E. ebbingei*) beneath the oak. The planting beneath the crab apple is St John's wort (*Hypericum calycinum*).

The azaleas beneath the bird cherries and in the private area of the garden are more exotic.

Nevertheless, these shrubs, particularly the ordinary yellow *mollis* or its white form, blend well with wilder ones.

The plant material in this garden is a good example of how decorative subjects can give way to native types as you move away from a house.

A GRASSY
EXHIBITION GARDEN

Once the concept of a 'garden' is broadened it is possible to find inspiration in all kinds of plant groupings, both wild and cultivated. This grassy garden by Bransford Nurseries, seen at the Welsh National Garden Festival in 1992, is pure sculpture. Furthermore, the bold and vigorous use of rockwork with gravel, aluminium piping and water is nothing short of inspirational.

It is not perhaps everyone's cup of tea – or even suited to the average location – but it is different and fun. It also shows how traditional materials can be integrated with modern ones, and how grassy native groupings can be interpreted by using more exotic forms. Both design and planting complement each other to create a brilliant overall concept.

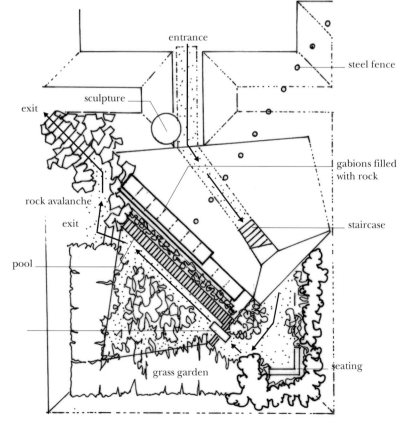

entrance

steel fence

sculpture

exit

gabions filled
with rock

rock avalanche

exit

staircase

pool

grass garden

seating

Above: The final explosion of this sculptured garden is of grasses, both native and introduced, among a placement of aluminium pipework.

The tall central grass mass is *Miscanthus sinensis*.

Left: There was a defined route around this small exhibition garden which was dug out of its site. Grass banks sloped up from the central decorative grass and water feature. The plan gives little indication of the interesting angles and materials of which the garden was constructed.

Right: This is surely a modern interpretation of a Welsh hillside. It shows how modern building materials can be combined with imaginative ground shaping, rock and, above all else, with a simple use of plant material. The bottom grass is *Carex pendula*, a native sedge for damp places, with, in the rows above, a fine fescue grass. The loose tumbling rock imitates scree and contrasts interestingly with the gabions that have been filled with rock to make stepped retaining walls.

PLANTING

GUIDE

The lists on the following pages cover the various aspects of how the plants that have been included may be used. They are a practical guide to putting plants in their rightful places – sites where they will grow naturally with no need for the intensive cultivation and maintenance demanded by more exotic species.

A pretty mass of heartsease
(*Viola tricolor*), which is both an
annual and biennial herb of
fields, hedgerows, waste
places and waysides.

The selection of plants on the following pages is necessarily a personal one. In making it I have kept as far as possible to native material, although there is always the question: 'When does an introduced species become a native?' This applies particularly to herbaceous material. At the end of the day I believe that one may include among native plantings introduced species that look in keeping. In other words, avoid anything that is definitely inappropriate to a country arrangement. Variegations must be out, as must strong gold or purple foliage. Broadly, our native forms are not very 'architectural' and their flowers are usually small with not many oranges and reds. Stick to species rather than cultivars. Finally, when making your selection let your soil type be your guide. It was the late Fred Streeter who said: 'The answer lies in the soil.' And it does.

LARGE DECIDUOUS TREES

	INLAND	COASTLAND	ACID	ALKALINE	CLAY	WINDBREAK INLAND	WINDBREAK COASTAL	AUTUMN COLOUR	FLOWERS	COPPICING	HEDGING	BERRIES HIPS CATKINS	SHADE
Acer pseudoplatanus SYCAMORE	•	•	•	•	•	•	•	•		•			
Carpinus betulus HORNBEAM	•	•		•	•	•		•		•	•		
Castanea sativa SWEET CHESTNUT	•	•		•	•	•	•	•		•			
Fagus sylvatica BEECH	•		•	•	•	•		•		•	•		
Fraxinus excelsior ASH	•	•		•	•	•	•			•			•
Populus tremula ASPEN	•	•	•	•	•	•		•		•			
Quercus cerris TURKEY OAK	•		•	•	•	•		•					
Quercus petraea SESSILE OAK	•		•		•	•		•					
Quercus robur COMMON OAK	•	•	•	•	•	•	•	•					
Salix alba WHITE WILLOW	•	•		•		•	•	•		•			
Tilia cordata SMALL LEAVED LIME	•			•	•	•		•					
Tilia platyphyllos LARGE LEAVED LIME	•			•	•								
Ulmus glabra WYCH ELM	•	•	•	•	•	•		•					
Ulmus procera/ U. minor vulgaris ENGLISH ELM	•		•	•	•			•					

MEDIUM DECIDUOUS TREES

	INLAND	COASTLAND	ACID	ALKALINE	CLAY	WINDBREAK INLAND	WINDBREAK COASTAL	AUTUMN COLOUR	FLOWERS	COPPICING	HEDGING	BERRIES HIPS CATKINS	SHADE
Acer campestre FIELD MAPLE	●			●	●			●			●		
Alnus glutinosa COMMON ALDER	●	●		●	●	●	●			●		●	
Alnus incana GREY ALDER	●			●		●				●		●	
Betula pendula BIRCH	●	●	●	●	●	●							
Juglans regia WALNUT	●		●	●								●	
Populus canescens GREY POPLAR	●		●	●		●	●	●					
Populus nigra BLACK POPLAR	●		●	●	●	●	●						
Prunus avium WILD CHERRY, GEAN	●			●	●			●	●				
Prunus padus BIRD CHERRY	●			●	●			●	●				
Salix fragilis CRACK WILLOW	●	●		●		●	●			●		●	
Sambucus nigra COMMON ELDER	●	●		●	●	●	●			●		●	●
Sorbus aria WHITEBEAM	●	●		●	●	●	●					●	
Sorbus aucuparia MOUNTAIN ASH, ROWAN	●	●	●	●	●			●				●	
Sorbus torminalis SERVICE TREE				●		●		●				●	

SMALL DECIDUOUS TREES

	INLAND	COASTLAND	ACID	ALKALINE	CLAY	WINDBREAK INLAND	WINDBREAK COASTAL	AUTUMN COLOUR	FLOWERS	COPPICING	HEDGING	BERRIES HIPS CATKINS	SHADE
Crataegus monogyna HAWTHORN	●	●		●		●	●	●	●		●		
Crataegus oxyacantha MAY, QUICK	●	●		●		●	●	●	●		●	●	

SMALL DECIDUOUS TREES

	INLAND	COASTLAND	ACID	ALKALINE	CLAY	WINDBREAK INLAND	WINDBREAK COASTAL	AUTUMN COLOUR	FLOWERS	COPPICING	HEDGING	BERRIES HIPS CATKINS	SHADE
Malus sylvestris CRAB APPLE	●		●	●	●			●	●		●	●	
Mespilus germanica MEDLAR	●			●				●	●			●	
Prunus cerasifera CHERRY PLUM, MYROBALAN	●			●				●	●		●	●	
Prunus cerasus SOUR CHERRY	●			●				●	●		●	●	
Prunus domestica WILD PLUM	●			●				●	●		●	●	
Prunus institita BULLACE	●			●				●	●		●	●	
Pyrus communis WILD PEAR	●			●				●	●		●	●	
Salix caprea GOAT WILLOW	●	●	●	●	●		●					●	
Salix cinerea GREY SALLOW	●	●	●	●	●		●					●	
Salix pentandra BAY WILLOW	●	●	●	●	●							●	
Salix viminalis COMMON OSIER	●	●	●	●	●		●			●		●	

LARGE EVERGREEN TREES

	INLAND	COASTLAND	ACID	ALKALINE	CLAY	WINDBREAK INLAND	WINDBREAK COASTAL	AUTUMN COLOUR	FLOWERS	COPPICING	HEDGING	BERRIES HIPS CATKINS	SHADE
Ilex aquifolium HOLLY	●	●	●	●	●	●					●	●	●
Pinus sylvestris SCOTS PINE	●	●	●			●							
Quercus ilex HOLM OAK	●	●	●	●	●	●	●				●		●
Taxus baccata YEW	●			●		●					●	●	●
Taxus baccata 'Fastigiata' IRISH YEW	●			●		●					●		●

LARGE DECIDUOUS SHRUBS

	INLAND	COASTLAND	ACID	ALKALINE	CLAY	WINDBREAK INLAND	WINDBREAK COASTAL	AUTUMN COLOUR	FLOWERS	COPPICING	HEDGING	BERRIES HIPS CATKINS	SHADE
Cornus alba RED-TWIGGED DOGWOOD	●		●	●	●	●		●		●			Light
Cornus sanguinea DOGWOOD	●		●	●	●	●		●		●			Light
Corylus avellana HAZEL	●		●	●	●	●				●		●	●
Cytisus scoparius BROOM	●	●	●	●	●	●	●		●				
Euonymus europaeus SPINDLE TREE	●	●	●	●	●	●					●	●	
Frangula alnus ALDER BUCKTHORN	●	●	●	●	●	●	●					●	
Hippophae rhamnoides SEA BUCKTHORN	●	●	●	●	●	●	●					●	
Prunus spinosa BLACKTHORN, SLOE	●	●	●	●	●	●	●	●	●		●	●	●
Rhamnus catharticas COMMON BUCKTHORN	●	●		●	●	●	●					●	
Rubus fruticosus BLACKBERRY	●	●	●	●	●	●						●	●
Salix purpurea PURPLE OSIER	●	●		●		●	●	●		●			
Ulex europaeus GORSE	●	●	●	●	●	●	●		●				
Viburnum lantana WAYFARING TREE	●			●	●	●		●			●	●	
Viburnum opulus GUELDER ROSE	●		●	●	●	●		●			●	●	Light

SMALL DECIDUOUS SHRUBS

	INLAND	COASTLAND	ACID	ALKALINE	CLAY	WINDBREAK INLAND	WINDBREAK COASTAL	AUTUMN COLOUR	FLOWERS	COPPICING	HEDGING	BERRIES HIPS CATKINS	SHADE
Calluna vulgaris LING HEATHER	●	●	●						●				
Erica cinerea BELL HEATHER	●	●	●						●				

SMALL DECIDUOUS SHRUBS

	INLAND	COASTLAND	ACID	ALKALINE	CLAY	WINDBREAK INLAND	WINDBREAK COASTAL	AUTUMN COLOUR	FLOWERS	COPPICING	HEDGING	BERRIES HIPS CATKINS	SHADE
Erica tetralix CROSS-LEAVED HEATH	●	●	●						●				
Hypericum androsaemum TUTSAN	●	●	●	●	●				●			●	●
Myrica gale BOG MYRTLE, GALE	●	●	●										
Symphoricarpos albus 'Laevigatus' SNOWBERRY	●	●	●	●	●	●						●	●

EVERGREEN SHRUBS

	INLAND	COASTLAND	ACID	ALKALINE	CLAY	WINDBREAK INLAND	WINDBREAK COASTAL	AUTUMN COLOUR	FLOWERS	COPPICING	HEDGING	BERRIES HIPS CATKINS	SHADE
Arbutus unedo KILLARNEY STRAWBERRY TREE	●	●	●						●			●	
Buxus sempervirens BOX	●			●	●	●					●		●
Daphne laureola SPURGE LAUREL	●			●					●			●	●
Ilex aquifolium COMMON HOLLY	●	●	●	●	●	●	●				●	●	●
Juniperus communis COMMON JUNIPER	●		●	●	●	●							●
Ligustrum vulgare PRIVET	●	●	●	●	●	●	●				●		●
Ruscus aculeatus BUTCHER'S BROOM	●			●		●							●
Vaccinium myrtillus BILBERRY	●	●	●									●	
Viburnum tinus LAURUSTINUS	●	●	●	●	●	●	●		●		●	●	●

CLIMBERS

	INLAND	COASTLAND	ACID	ALKALINE	CLAY	WINDBREAK INLAND	WINDBREAK COASTAL	AUTUMN COLOUR	FLOWERS	COPPICING	HEDGING	BERRIES HIPS CATKINS	SHADE
Clematis vitalba TRAVELLER'S JOY, OLD MAN'S BEARD	●	●	●	●	●				●				
Hedera helix COMMON IVY	●	●	●	●	●								●
Humulus lupulus HOP	●	●	●	●	●			●	●				
Lathyrus sylvestris EVERLASTING PEA	●		●	●	●				●				
Lonicera periclymenum HONEYSUCKLE, WOODBINE	●	●	●	●	●				●				●

ROSES

	INLAND	COASTLAND	ACID	ALKALINE	CLAY	WINDBREAK INLAND	WINDBREAK COASTAL	AUTUMN COLOUR	FLOWERS	COPPICING	HEDGING	BERRIES HIPS CATKINS	SHADE
Rosa arvensis FIELD ROSE	●		●	●	●	●			●		●	●	
Rosa canina DOG ROSE	●	●	●	●	●	●	●		●		●	●	
Rosa macrantha	●		●	●	●	●			●		●	●	
Rosa rubiginosa SWEET BRIAR, EGLANTINE	●	●	●	●	●	●	●		●		●	●	
Rosa spinosissima SCOTCH, BURNET ROSE	●	●	●	●	●	●	●		●		●	●	●
Rosa villosa APPLE ROSE	●		●	●	●	●			●		●	●	

NATIVE WILD FLOWERS FOR THE GARDEN

	MEADOW FULL SUN	DAMP SHADE WOODLAND	DRY SHADE	WATERSIDE	ACID	ALKALINE	FLOWERING TIMES MAR-MAY	MAY-JUNE	JUNE-SEPT	HEIGHTS LESS THAN 30 CM (12 IN)	30–60 CM (12–24 IN)	OVER 60 CM (24 IN)
Achillea millefolium YARROW P	●				●	●		●	●			●
Agrostemma githago CORNCOCKLE A	●				●	●			●			●

A × annual; B × biennial; P × perennial

	MEADOW FULL SUN	DAMP SHADE WOODLAND	DRY SHADE	WATERSIDE	ACID	ALKALINE	FLOWERING TIMES			HEIGHTS		
							MAR-MAY	MAY-JUNE	JUNE-SEPT	LESS THAN 30 CM (12 IN)	30–60 CM (12–24 IN)	OVER 60 CM (24 IN)
Ajuga reptans BUGLE P	●	●		●	●			●		●		
Alchemilla vulgaris LADY'S MANTLE P	●	●			●	●			●		●	
Aquilegia vulgaris COLUMBINE P	●	●	●		●			●				●
Arum maculatum LORDS AND LADIES, CUCKOO PINT P		●		●	●	●	●				●	
Caltha palustris MARSH MARIGOLD P		●		●	●			●				●
Campanula glomerata CLUSTERED BELLFLOWER P	●				●		●	●	●			●
Campanula rotundifolia HAREBELL P	●		●		●	●			●	●		
Cardamine pratensis CUCKOO FLOWER P	●	●		●	●	●	●	●	●		●	
Centaurea cyanus CORNFLOWER A	●				●	●		●				●
Centaurea scabiosa GREATER KNAPWEED P	●				●	●			●			●
Centranthus ruber RED VALERIAN P	●		●		●	●		●	●			●
Conopodium majus PIGNUT P	●		●		●	●		●			●	
Dianthus gratianopolitanus CHEDDAR PINK P	●				●	●			●	●		
Digitalis purpurea FOXGLOVE B		●	●		●				●			●
Dipsacus fullonum TEASEL B	●				●	●			●			●
Epilobium angustifolium ROSEBAY WILLOW HERB P	●	●	●		●	●			●			●
Euphorbia amygdaloides WOOD SPURGE P		●	●		●	●	●				●	
Euphorbia lathyris CAPER SPURGE B		●	●		●	●	●				●	

NATIVE WILD FLOWERS FOR THE GARDEN

	MEADOW FULL SUN	DAMP SHADE WOODLAND	DRY SHADE	WATERSIDE	ACID	ALKALINE	FLOWERING TIMES			HEIGHTS		
							MAR-MAY	MAY-JUNE	JUNE-SEPT	LESS THAN 30 CM (12 IN)	30-60 CM (12-24 IN)	OVER 60 CM (24 IN)
Filipendula vulgaris DROPWORT P	●			●	●	●		●	●			●
Fragaria vesca WILD STRAWBERRY P	●		●		●	●	●	●	●	●		
Galium odoratum WOODRUFF P		●				●		●			●	
Galium verum LADY'S BEDSTRAW P	●				●	●			●		●	
Geranium phaeum DUSKY CRANESBILL P		●	●		●	●		●			●	
Geranium pratense MEADOW CRANESBILL P	●		●						●			●
Geranium sanguineum BLOODY CRANESBILL P	●					●		●	●		●	
Geum rivale WATER AVENS P		●		●	●	●	●	●			●	
Helleborus foetidus STINKING HELLEBORE		●				●	Jan-Feb				●	
Hypericum maculatum IMPERFORATE ST JOHNS WORT P		●			●	●			●		●	
Inula helenium ELECAMPANE P	●				●	●			●			●
Knautia arvensis FIELD SCABIOUS P	●				●	●			●			●
Lamiastrum galeobdolon YELLOW ARCHANGEL P		●	●		●			●			●	
Leucanthemum vulgare OX-EYE DAISY P	●				●	●		●	●			●
Lychnis flos-cuculi RAGGED ROBIN CAMPION P		●	●	●	●	●		●			●	
Lysimachia vulgaris YELLOW STRIFE P	●			●	●	●			●			●
Lythrum salicaria PURPLE LOOSESTRIFE P	●	●		●	●	●			●			●
Malva moschata MUSK MALLOW P	●		●		●	●			●		●	

NATIVE WILD FLOWERS FOR THE GARDEN

	MEADOW FULL SUN	DAMP SHADE WOOD-LAND	DRY SHADE	WATER-SIDE	ACID	ALKALINE	FLOWERING TIMES MAR-MAY	MAY-JUNE	JUNE-SEPT	HEIGHTS LESS THAN 30 CM (12 IN)	30–60 CM (12–24 IN)	OVER 60 CM (24 IN)
Mentha aquatica WATER MINT P	●	●		●	●	●			●			●
Myosotis scorpioides WATER FORGET-ME-NOT P		●		●	●	●		●	●		●	
Myrrhis odorata SWEET CICELY P		●			●	●		●				●
Oenothera biennis COMMON EVENING PRIMROSE B	●				●	●			●			●
Onopordum acanthum SCOTCH THISTLE P	●				●	●		●				●
Papaver rhoeas COMMON POPPY A	●				●	●		●	●		●	
Polemonium caeruleum JACOB'S LADDER P	●				●	●		●	●		●	
Polygonatum multiflorum SOLOMON'S SEAL P		●						●				●
Primula veris COWSLIP P	●	●			●	●	●				●	
Primula vulgaris PRIMROSE P		●			●	●	●				●	
Prunella vulgaris SELF-HEAL P	●				●	●			●		●	
Pulmonaria officinalis LUNGWORT P		●		●	●			●	●		●	
Ranunculus acris MEADOW BUTTERCUP P	●				●	●	●	●			●	
Ranunculus ficaria LESSER CELANDINE P		●			●		●			●		
Rumex hydrolapathum WATER DOCK P			●	●	●				●			●
Salvia pratensis MEADOW CLARY P	●				●	●			●			●
Saponaria officinalis SOAPWORT P	●				●				●			●
Saxifraga oppositifolia PURPLE SAXIFRAGE P	●				●	●	●			●		

NATIVE WILD FLOWERS FOR THE GARDEN

	MEADOW FULL SUN	DAMP SHADE WOOD-LAND	DRY SHADE	WATER-SIDE	ACID	ALKALINE	FLOWERING TIMES MAR-MAY	MAY-JUNE	JUNE-SEPT	HEIGHTS LESS THAN 30 CM (12 IN)	30–60 CM (12–24 IN)	OVER 60 CM (24 IN)
Silene vulgaris BLADDER CAMPION P	●	●			●			●	●		●	
Silybum marianum MILK THISTLE P	●				●	●		●				●
Solidago virgaurea GOLDEN ROD P	●		●		●	●			●		●	
Stachys officinalis BETONY P	●		●		●	●			●		●	
Tanacetum parthenium FEVERFEW P	●				●				●		●	
Trollius europaeus GLOBE FLOWER P	●	●		●	●	●			●		●	
Verbascum nigrum DARK MULLEIN B	●				●	●			●			●
Veronica chamaedrys GERMANDER SPEEDWELL P	●		●		●	●	●	●	●		●	
Vinca minor BLUE PERIWINKLE P		●	●		●	●	●			●		
Viola odorata SWEET VIOLET P	●	●	●	●	●	●	Feb-April			●		
Viola riviniana COMMON DAY VIOLET P		●			●	●	●	●	●	●		

NATIVE BULBS

	MEADOW FULL SUN	DAMP SHADE WOOD-LAND	DRY SHADE	WATER-SIDE	ACID	ALKALINE	FLOWERING TIMES MAR-MAY	MAY-JUNE	JUNE-SEPT	HEIGHTS LESS THAN 30 CM (12 IN)	30–60 CM (12–24 IN)	OVER 60 CM (23 IN)
Allium ursinum RAMSON, WILD GARLIC		●			●	●	●	●			●	
Anemone nemorosa WOOD ANEMONE		●			●	●	●			●		
Colchicum autumnale AUTUMN CROCUS	●	●			●	●			Aug-Oct	●		
Convallaria majalis LILY OF THE VALLEY		●	●		●	●		●		●		
Crocus nudiflorus	●				●	●			Sept-Oct	●		

NATIVE BULBS

	MEADOW FULL SUN	DAMP SHADE WOODLAND	DRY SHADE	WATERSIDE	ACID	ALKALINE	FLOWERING TIMES MAR-MAY	MAY-JUNE	JUNE-SEPT	HEIGHTS LESS THAN 30 CM (12 IN)	30–60 CM (12–24 IN)	OVER 60 CM (23 IN)
Crocus vernus SPRING CROCUS	●	●	●		●	●	●			●		
Eranthis hyemalis WINTER ACONITE		●			●		Jan-March			●		
Fritillaria meleagris SNAKES HEAD FRITILLARY	●	●		●	●	●	●				●	
Galanthus nivalis SNOWDROP		●	●		●	●	Jan-Mar			●		
Iris foetidissima GLADDON		●	●	●	●	●						●
Iris pseudacorus YELLOW IRIS				●	●	●		●	●			●
Leucojum aestivum SUMMER SNOWFLAKE		●	●		●	●					●	
Leucojum vernum SPRING SNOWFLAKE		●	●		●	●	Feb-April				●	
Narcissus poeticus PHEASANT'S EYE	●				●		●				●	
Narcissus pseudonarcissus LENT LILY	●	●			●	●	Feb-April				●	
Narcissus pseudonarcissus obvallaris TENBY DAFFODIL	●	●			●	●	Feb-April				●	
Scilla non-scripta BLUEBELL		●			●	●		●			●	

NATIVE FERNS

	MEADOW FULL SUN	DAMP SHADE WOODLAND	DRY SHADE	WATERSIDE	ACID	ALKALINE	FLOWERING TIMES MAR-MAY	MAY-JUNE	JUNE-SEPT	HEIGHTS LESS THAN 30 CM (12 IN)	30–60 CM (12–24 IN)	OVER 60 CM (24 IN)
Adiantum capillus-veneris MAIDENHAIR		●	●		●	●					●	
Asplenium scolopendrium HART'S TONGUE		●	●	●							●	
Athyrium filix-femina LADY'S FERN		●	●									●

NATIVE FERNS

	MEADOW FULL SUN	DAMP SHADE WOODLAND	DRY SHADE	WATER-SIDE	ACID	ALKALINE	FLOWERING TIMES			HEIGHTS		
							MAR-MAY	MAY-JUNE	JUNE-SEPT	LESS THAN 30 CM (12 IN)	30–60 CM (12–24 IN)	OVER 60 CM (24 IN)
Dryopteris filix-mas MALE FERN		●	●	●	●	●						●
Gymnocarpium dryopteris OAK FERN		●			●	●					●	
Osmunda regalis ROYAL FERN		●		●	●	●						●
Polypodium vulgare 'Cornubiense'		●			●	●					●	
Polystichum aculeatum HARD SHIELD FERN		●	●		●	●						●

NATIVE GRASSES, SEDGES AND RUSHES

	MEADOW FULL SUN	DAMP SHADE WOODLAND	DRY SHADE	WATER-SIDE	ACID	ALKALINE	FLOWERING TIMES			HEIGHTS		
							MAR-MAY	MAY-JUNE	JUNE-SEPT	LESS THAN 30 CM (12 IN)	30–60 CM (12–24 IN)	OVER 60 CM (24 IN)
Briza media QUAKING GRASS	●				●	●					●	
Carex pendula WEEPING SEDGE		●		●	●	●		●				●
Carex pseudocyperus CYPRUS SEDGE				●	●	●			●		●	
Carex riparia GREATER POND SEDGE				●	●	●					●	
Cyperus longus GALINGALE				●	●	●			●			●
Deschampsia caespitosa TUFTED HAIR GRASS	●			●	●	●			●			●
Eriophorum angustifolium COTTON GRASS				●	●	●		●			●	
Festuca arundinacea TALL FESCUE	●				●	●			●			●
Juncus effusus SOFT RUSH				●	●	●		●	●			●
Luzula sylvatica GREAT WOODRUSH		●		●	●	●		●				●

BIBLIOGRAPHY

BECKETT, KENNETH and GILLIAN *Planting Native Trees and Shrubs,* Jarrold.

BISGROVE, RICHARD *The Gardens of Gertrude Jekyll,* Francis Lincoln, 1992.

BRIGDEN, ROY *Ploughs and Ploughing,* Shire, 1984.

BROOKS, ALAN *Woodlands,* British Trust for Conservation Volunteers, 1980.

BRUNSKILL, R. W. *Traditional Buildings of Britain,* Victor Gollancz, 1986.

CHAMBERS, JOHN *Wild Flower Gardening,* WI Books, 1989.

CLAY, CHRISTOPHER (ed.) *Rural Society: landowners, peasants and labourers 1500–1750,* Cambridge University Press, 1990.

COLEBOURN, PHIL and GIBBONS, BOB *Britain's Countryside Heritage,* Blandford in association with The National Trust, 1990.

COLVIN, BRENDA *Land and Landscape,* Murray, 1948.

CROWE, SYLVIA and MITCHELL, MARY *The Pattern of Landscape,* Packard, 1988.

DARLEY, GILLIAN and TOLER, PAMELA *The National Trust Book of the Farm,* Weidenfeld & Nicolson, 1981.

JOYCE, DAVID *The English Garden Tradition,* Century, 1987.

DRABBLE, MARGARET *A Writer's Britain,* Thames and Hudson, 1979.

DUTTON, RALPH *The English Garden,* Batsford, 1937.

FERGUSON, MIKE and CLARK, COLIN *Understanding Weather and Climate,* Macmillan, 1984.

FLADMARK, J. M., MULVAGH, G. Y. and EVANS, B. M. *Tomorrow's Architectural Heritage,* Mainstream Publishing, 1991.

FRANCK, GERTRUD *Companion Planting,* Aquarian Press, 1983.

GATES, PHILIP *Spring Fever,* HarperCollins, 1992.

GRAYSON, ANNA *Rock Solid: Britain's most ancient heritage,* The Natural History Museum, 1992.

GREEN, BRYN *Countryside Conservation,* Allen and Unwin, 1985.

HARVEY, NIGEL *Trees, Woods and Forests,* Shire, 1981.

HEWISON, ROBERT *The Heritage Industry,* Methuen, 1987.

HOSKINS, W. G. *English Landscapes* BBC, 1973.

HYAMS, EDWARD *English Cottage Gardens,* Whittet Books, 1986.

JEKYLL, GERTRUDE *Wood and Garden,* Longmans, 1901.

LANCASTER, MICHAEL *Britain in View,* Quiller Press, 1984.

MABEY, RICHARD *The Common Ground,* Dent, 1993.

MASSINGHAM, BETTY *Miss Jekyll: Portrait of a Great Gardener,* Country Life Books, 1966.

MOLLISON, BILL *Introduction to Permaculture,* Tagari, 1991.

MORLAND, JOANNA for Common Ground, *New Milestones,* 1993.

The Patchwork Landscape, Reader's Digest, 1984.

PHILLIPS, ROGER *Wild Flowers of Britain,* Pan Books, 1977.

POLLAN, MICHAEL *Second Nature,* The Atlantic Monthly Press, 1991.

RACKHAM, OLIVER *Trees and Woodland in the British Landscape,* Dent, 1976.

REINHARDT, THOMAS A., REINHARDT, MARTINA and MOSKOWITZ, MARK *Ornamental Grass Gardening,* Macdonald Orbis, 1989.

TAYLOR, CHRISTOPHER *Fields in the English Landscape,* Dent, 1982.

WHITLOCK, RALPH *The English Farm,* Dent, 1983.

WILSON, RON *Back Garden Wildlife Sanctuary,* Penguin 1981.

SOME NATIVE PLANT NURSERIES

TREES AND SHRUBS

BTCV Trees
Plashett Wood, Rosehill, Isfield,
Uckfield, East Sussex, TN22 5VQ
TEL: 0825 750244

Kingsfield Conservation Nursery
Broadenham Lane, Winsham,
Chard, Somerset, TA20 4JF
TEL: 0460 30070

WILD FLOWER PLANTS

The Wildflower Centre
Church Farm, Sisland, Loddon,
Norwich, Norfolk, NR14 6EF
TEL: 0508 235

The Wildlife Gardening Centre
Witney Road, Kingston Bagpuize,
Abingdon, Oxfordshire, OX13 5AN
TEL: 0865 821660

Kingsfield Conservation Nursery
Broadenham Lane, Winsham,
Chard, Somerset, TA20 4JF
TEL: 0460 30070

John Chambers
15 Westleigh Road,
Barton Seagrave, Kettering,
Northamptonshire, NN15 5AJ
TEL: 0933 681632

Donald MacIntyre, Emorsgate
Seeds
Emorsgate, Terrington
St Clement, King's Lynn,
Norfolk, PE34 4NY
TEL: 0553 829028

BTCV Wildflowers
Plashett Wood, Rosehill, Isfield,
Uckfield, East Sussex, TN22 5VQ
TEL: 0825 750244

DECORATIVE GRASSES

Trevor Scott
Thorpe Park Cottage, Thorpe-le-
Soken, Essex, CP16 0HN
TEL: 0255 861308

Kingsfield Conservation Nursery
Broadenham Lane, Winsham,
Chard, Somerset, TA20 4JF
TEL: 0460 30070

Emorsgate Seeds
Emorsgate, Terrington
St Clement, King's Lynn,
Norfolk, PE34 4NY
TEL: 0553 829028

HARDY FERNS

T & D Marston
Culag, Green Lane, Nafferton,
East Yorkshire, YO25 0LF
TEL: 0377 254487

Fibrex Nurseries Ltd
Honeybourne Road, Pebworth,
Nr. Stratford-upon-Avon,
CV37 8XT
TEL: 0789 720788

NATIVE BULBS

John Shipton
Y Felin, Henllan Amgoed,
Whitland, Dyfed SA34 0SL
TEL: 0994 240125

INDEX